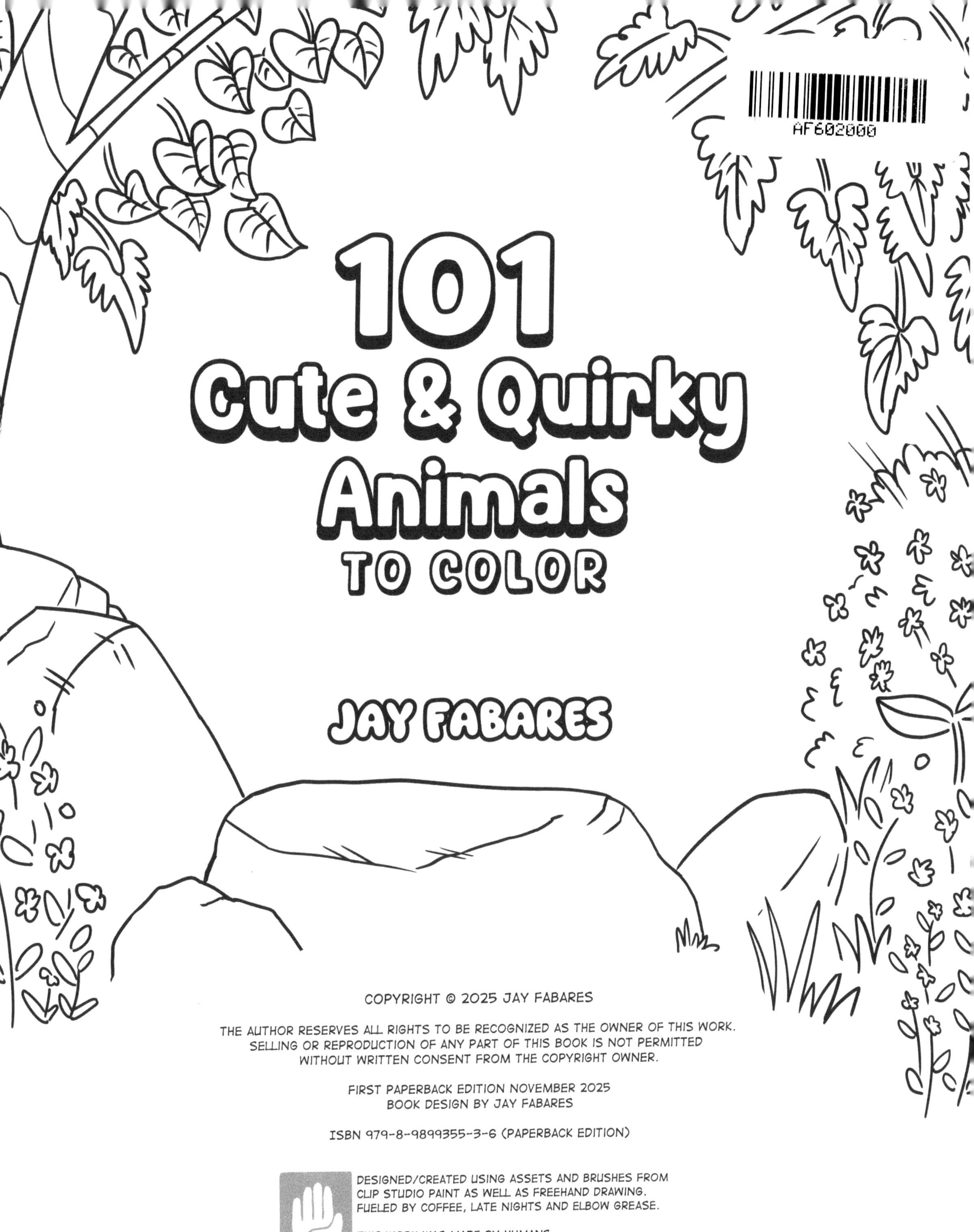

101 Cute & Quirky Animals to Color

JAY FABARES

FIRST PAPERBACK EDITION NOVEMBER 2025
BOOK DESIGN BY JAY FABARES

ISBN 979-8-9899355-3-6 (PAPERBACK EDITION)

HUMAN MADE

DESIGNED/CREATED USING ASSETS AND BRUSHES FROM CLIP STUDIO PAINT AS WELL AS FREEHAND DRAWING. FUELED BY COFFEE, LATE NIGHTS AND ELBOW GREASE.

THIS WORK WAS MADE BY HUMANS. NO AI OR MACHINE GENERATED WORKS ARE INCLUDED IN THIS PROJECT. BY SUPPORTING THIS PROJECT YOU ARE SUPPORTING REAL HUMAN BEINGS WHO HAVE DREAMS, PASSIONS, & BILLS. THANK YOU.

HUMAN MADE ICON BY HINOKODO

THIS COLORING BOOK BELONGS TO

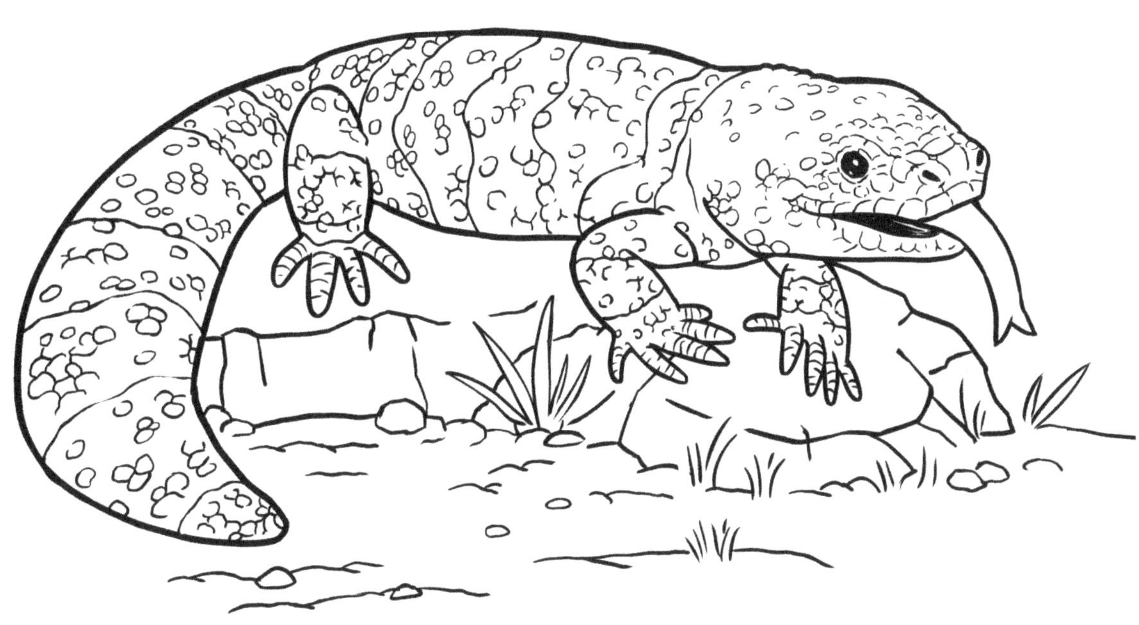

place a paper behind the coloring page
to prevent further bleed-through

aardvark

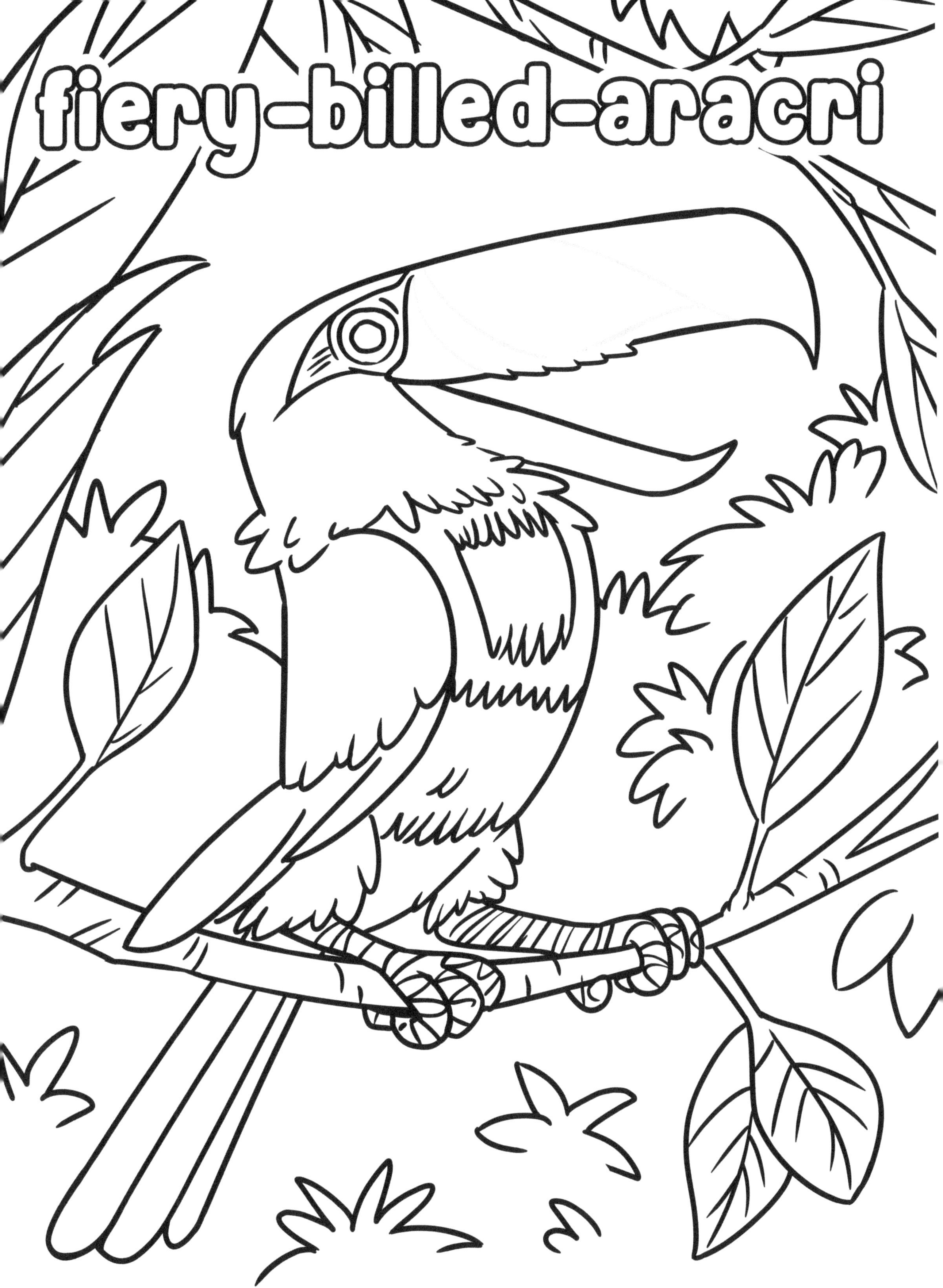
fiery-billed-aracri

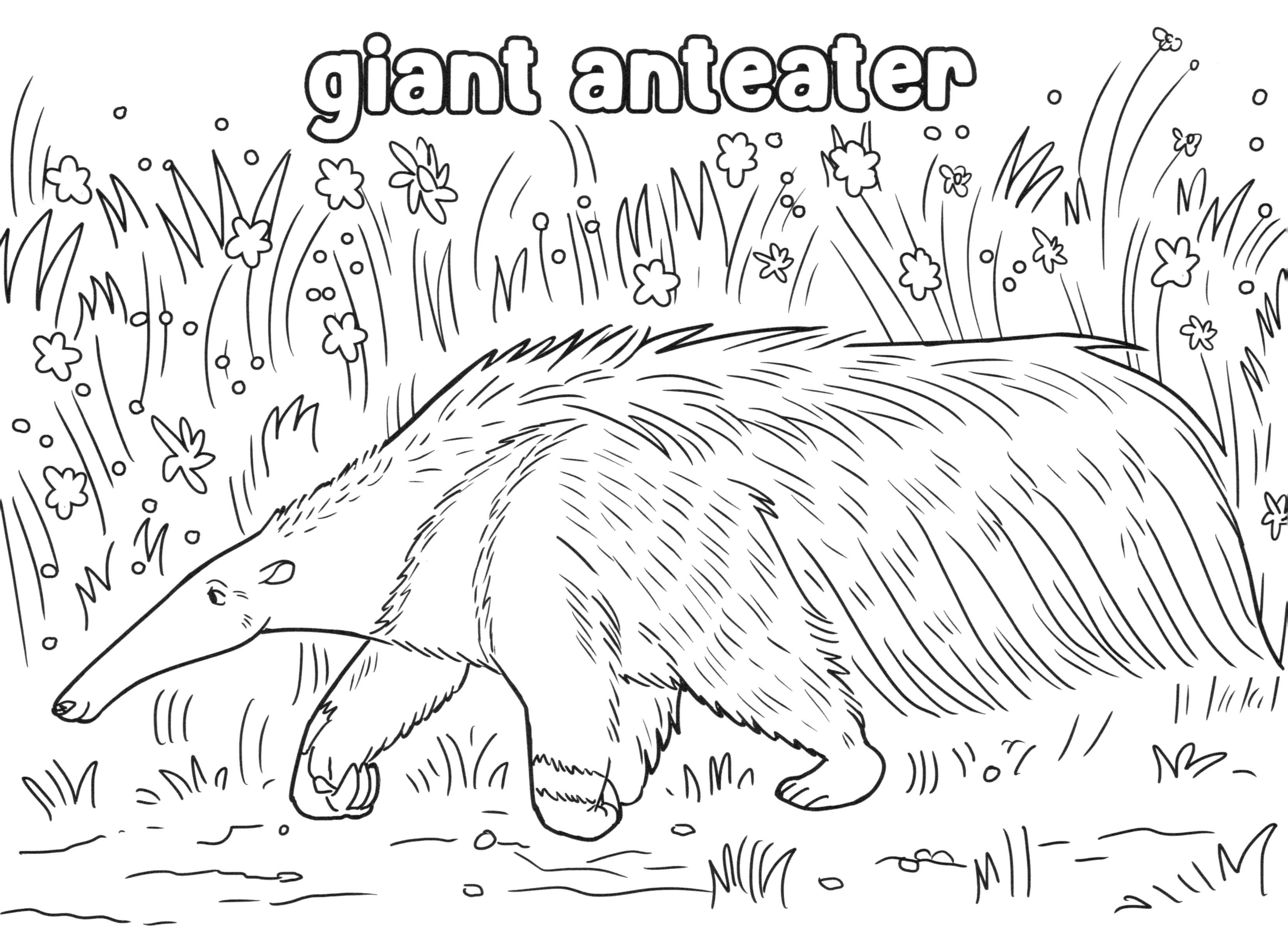
giant anteater

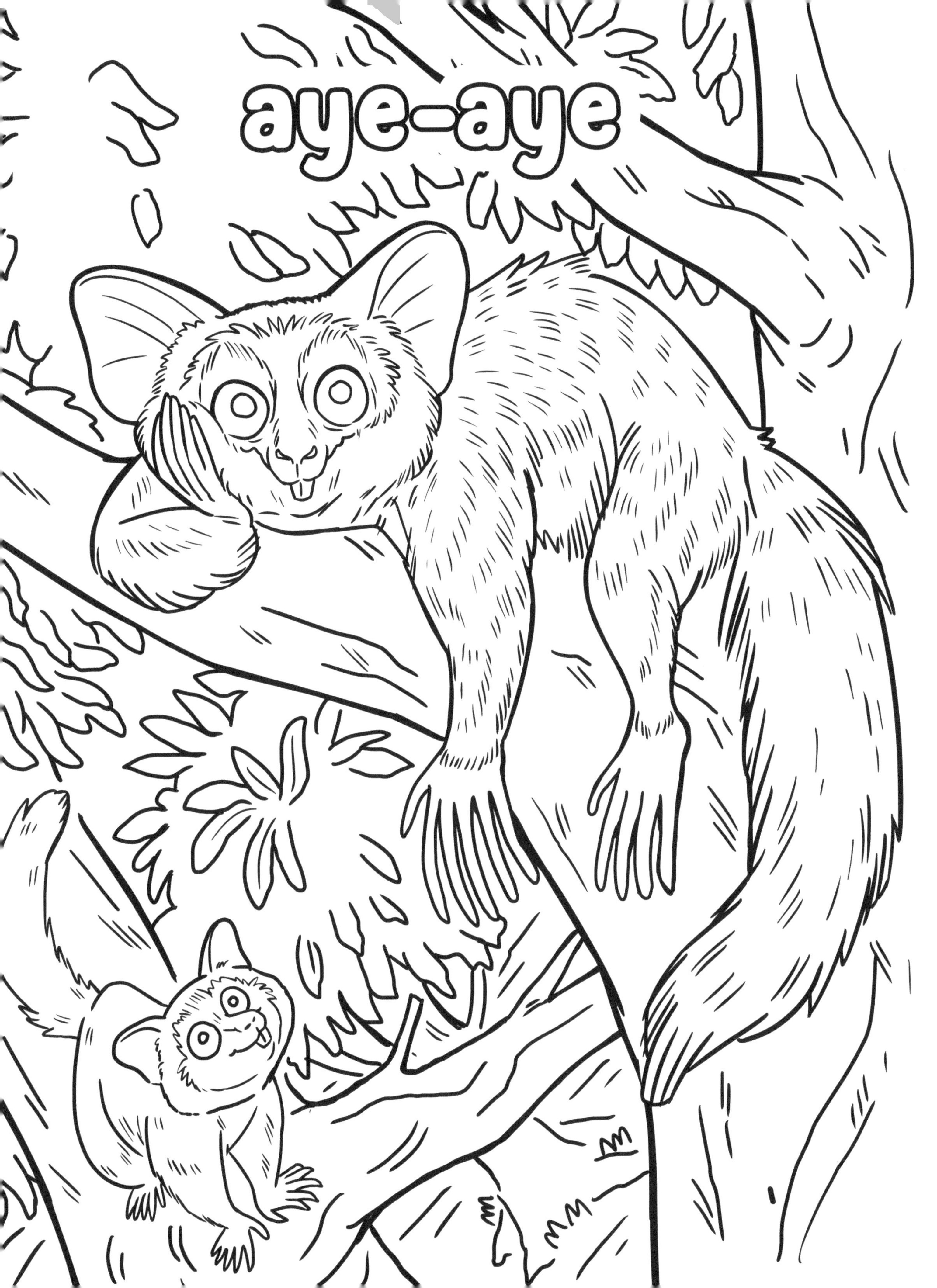
aye-aye

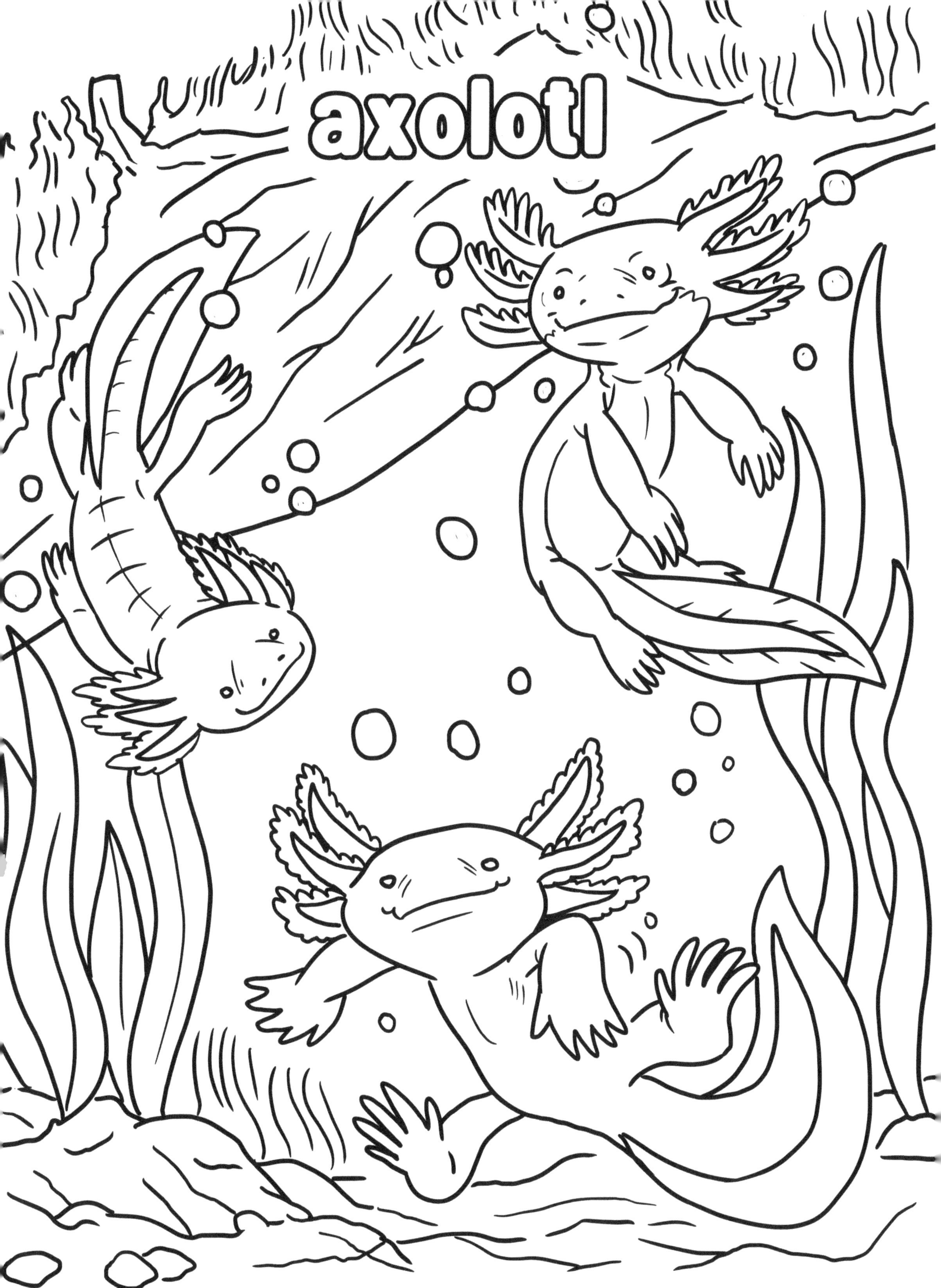
axolotl

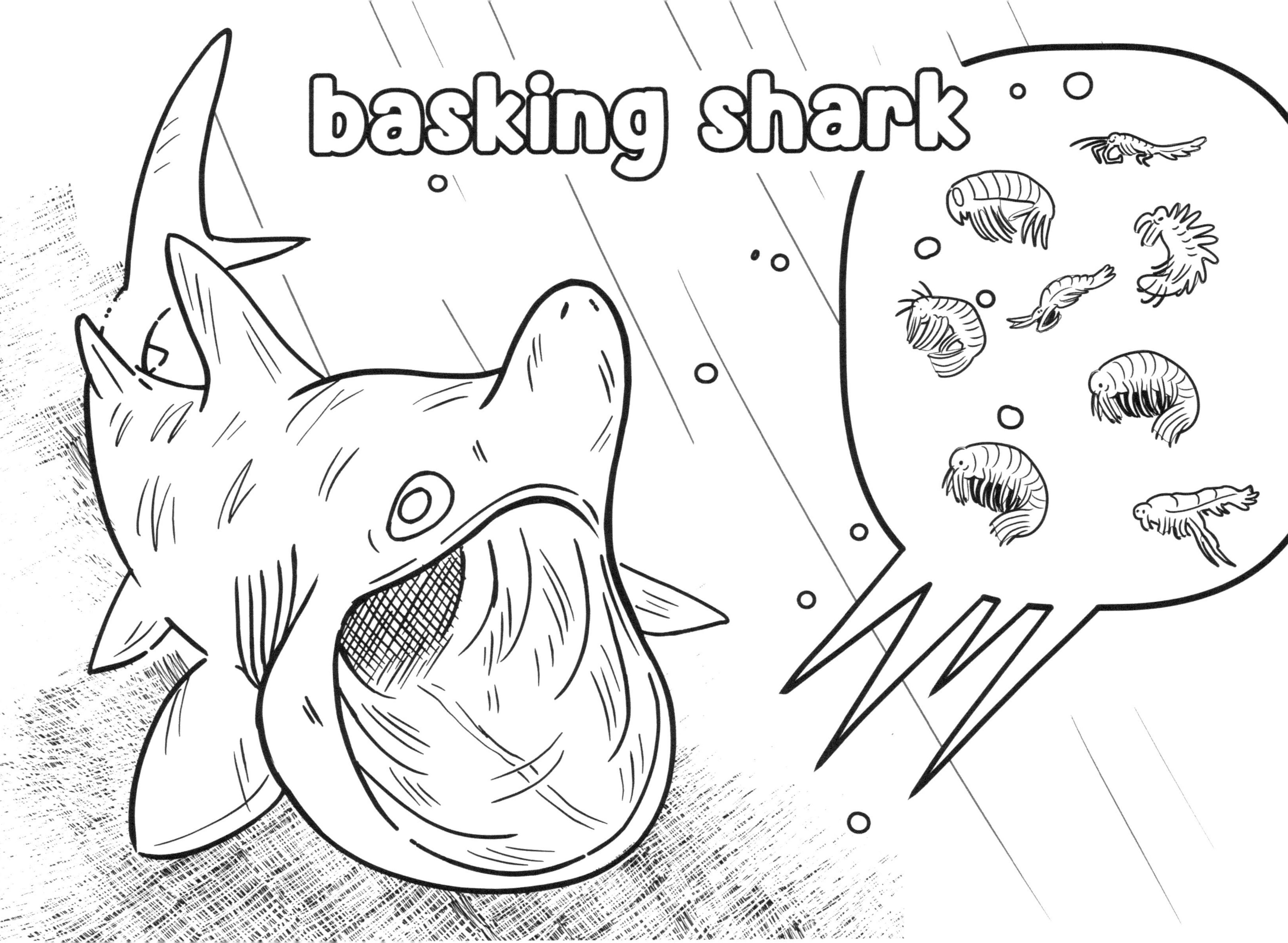
basking shark

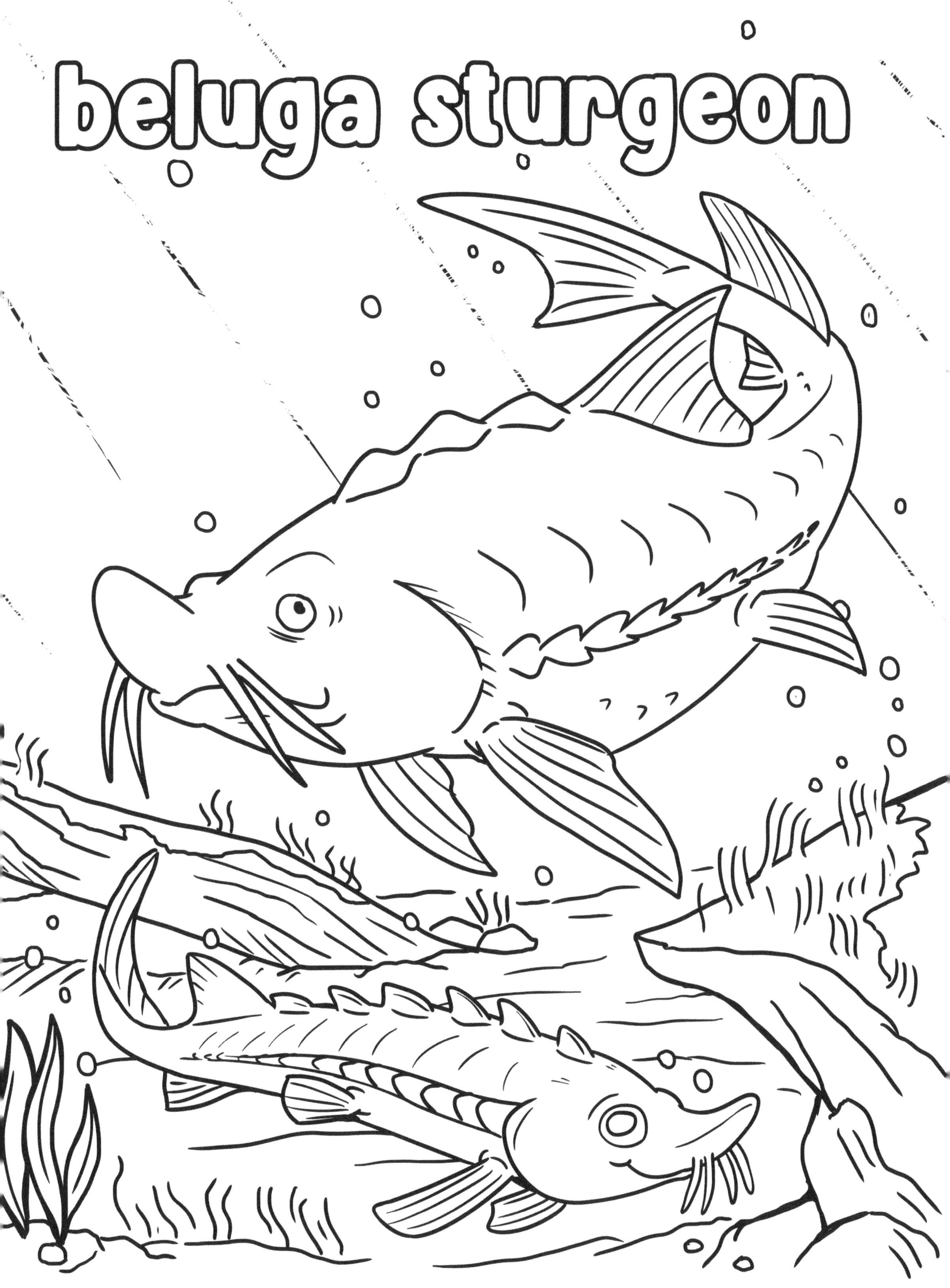
beluga sturgeon

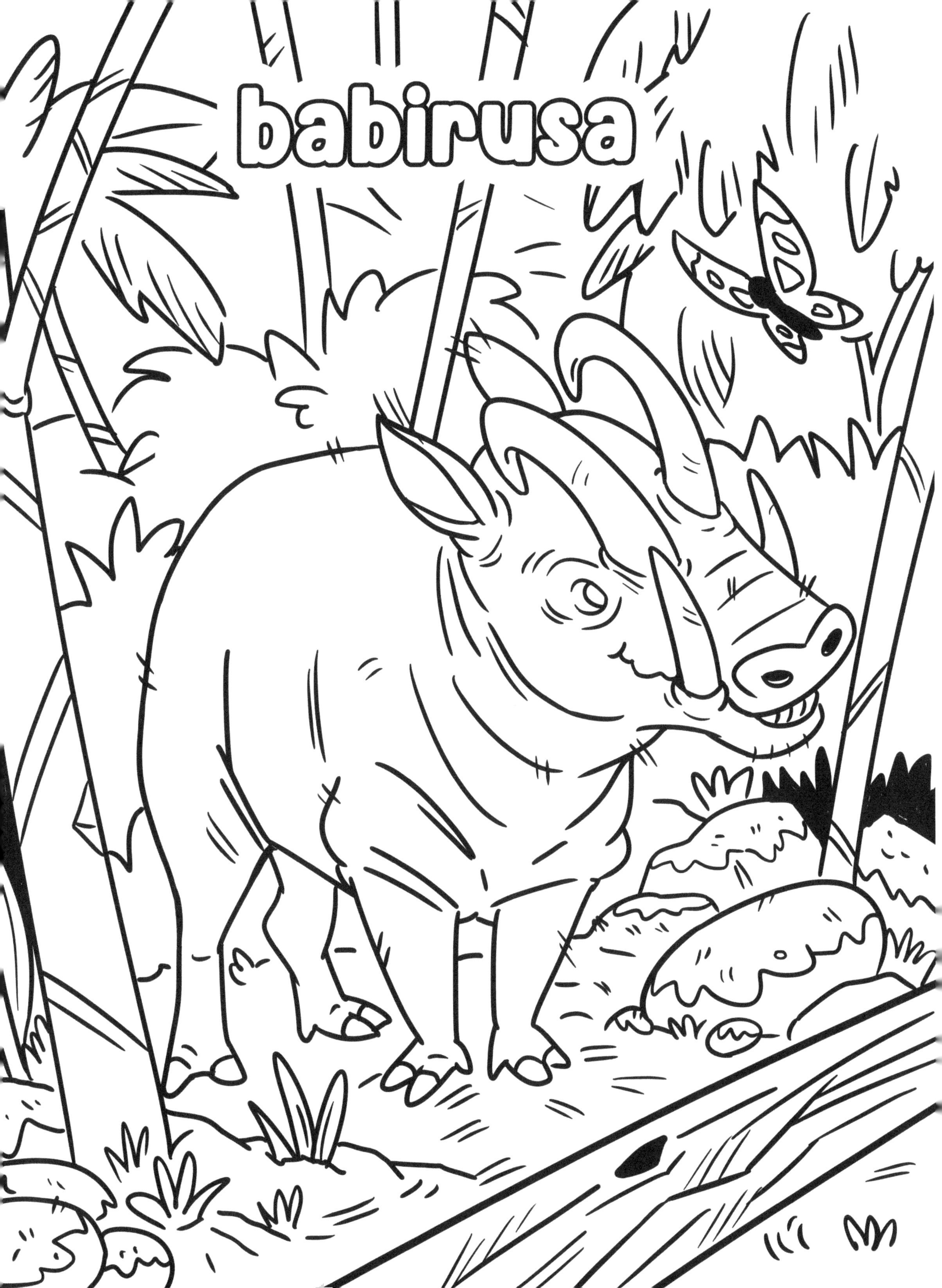
babirusa

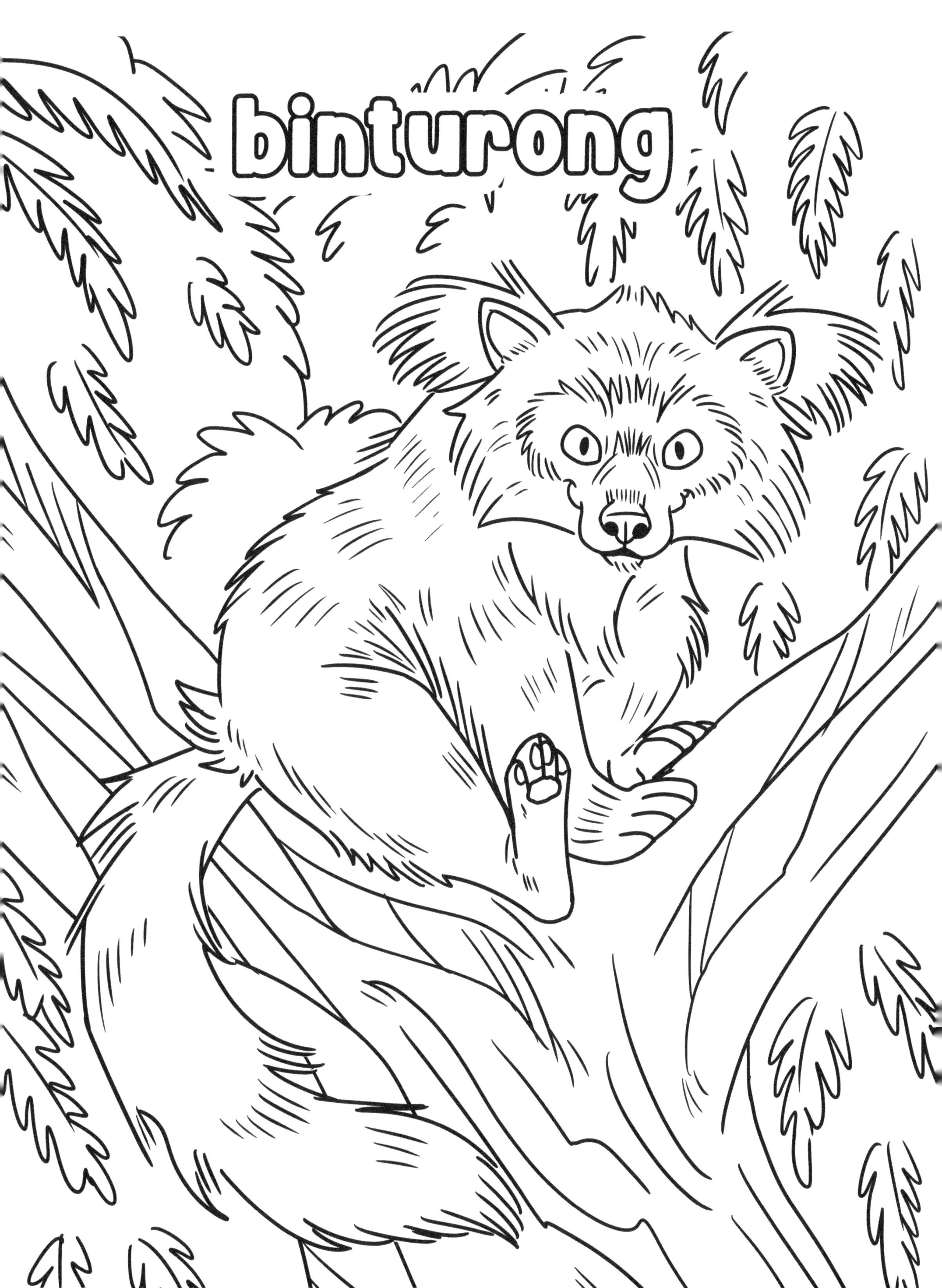
binturong

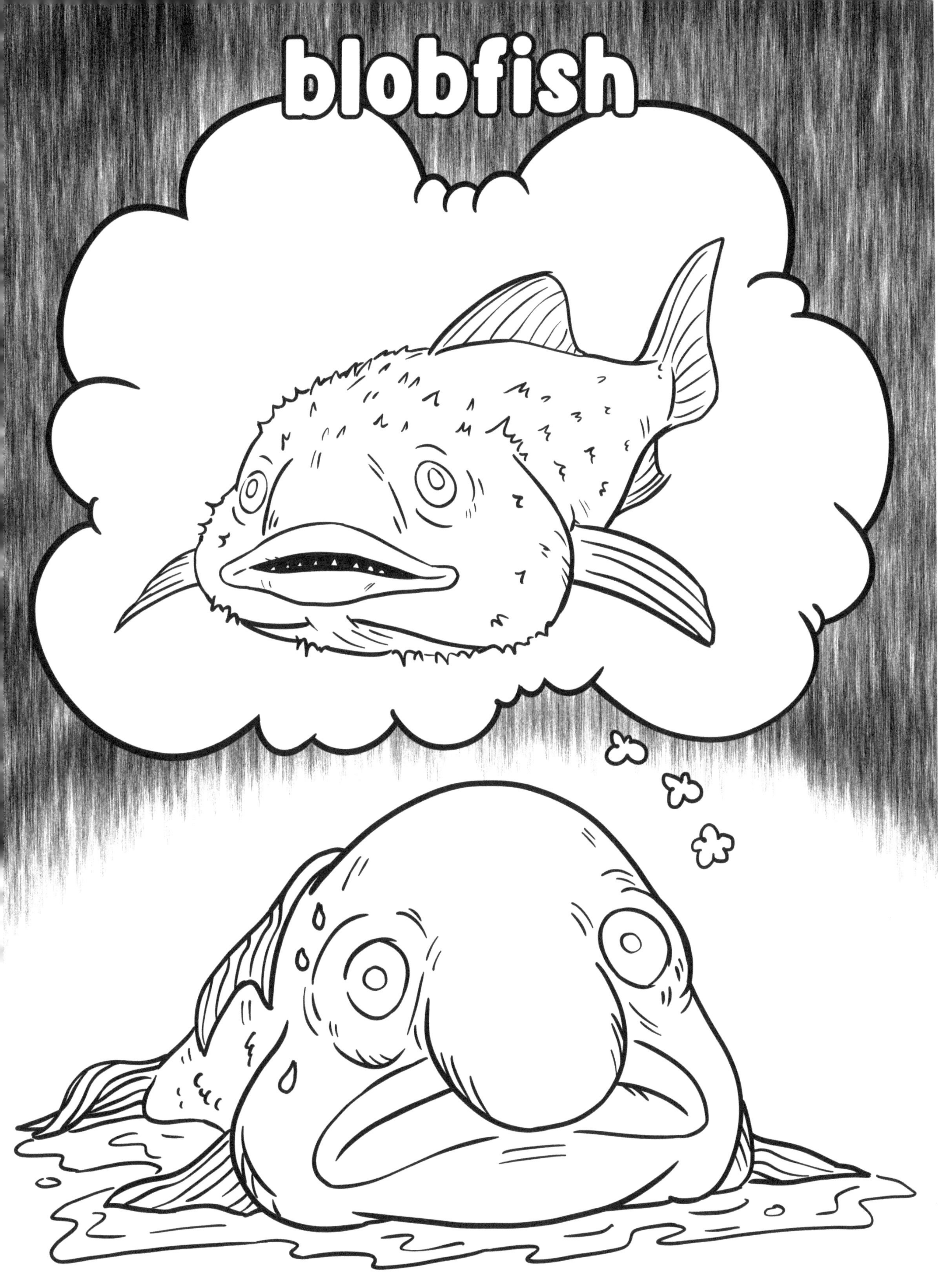
blobfish

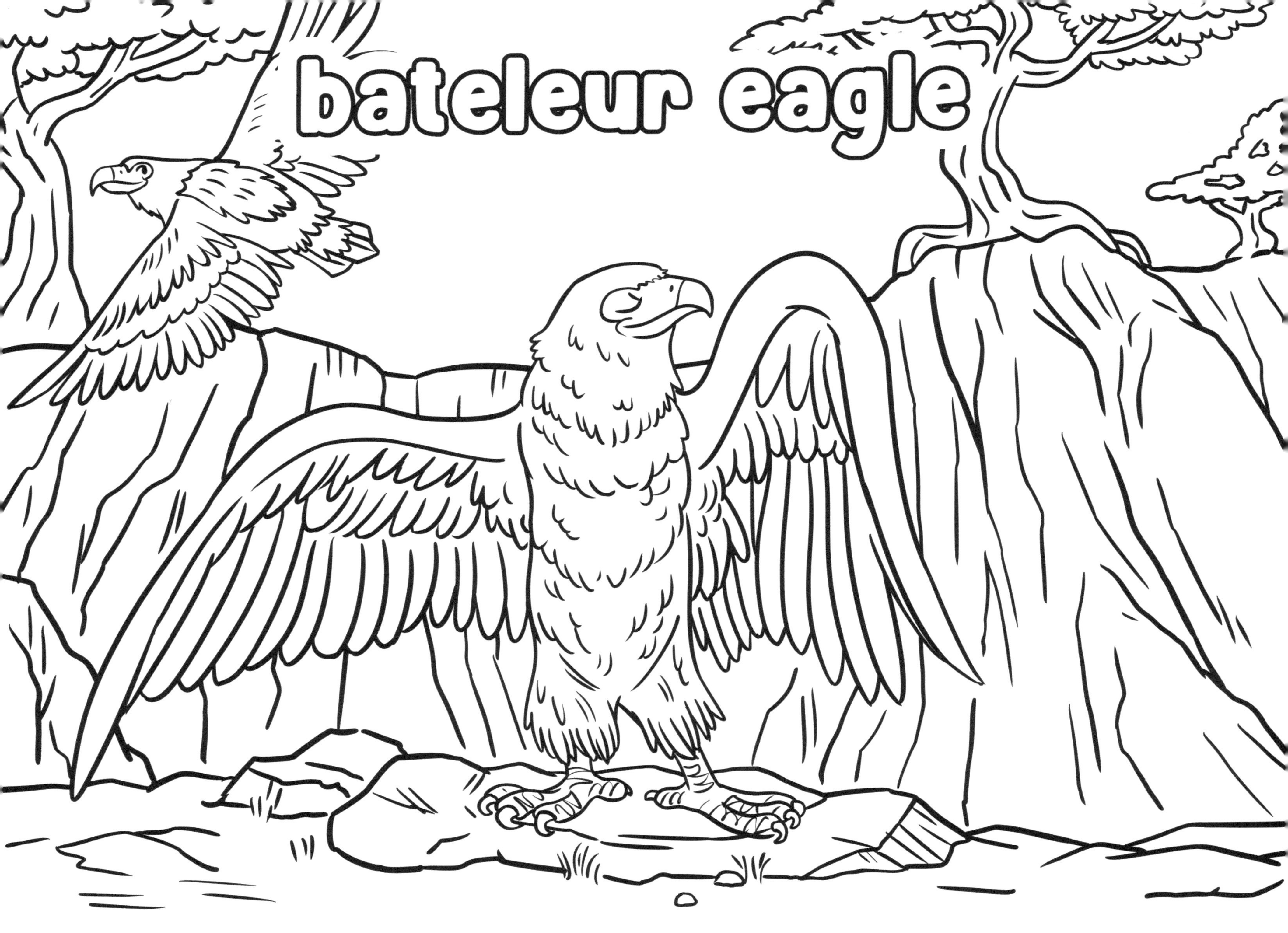
bateleur eagle

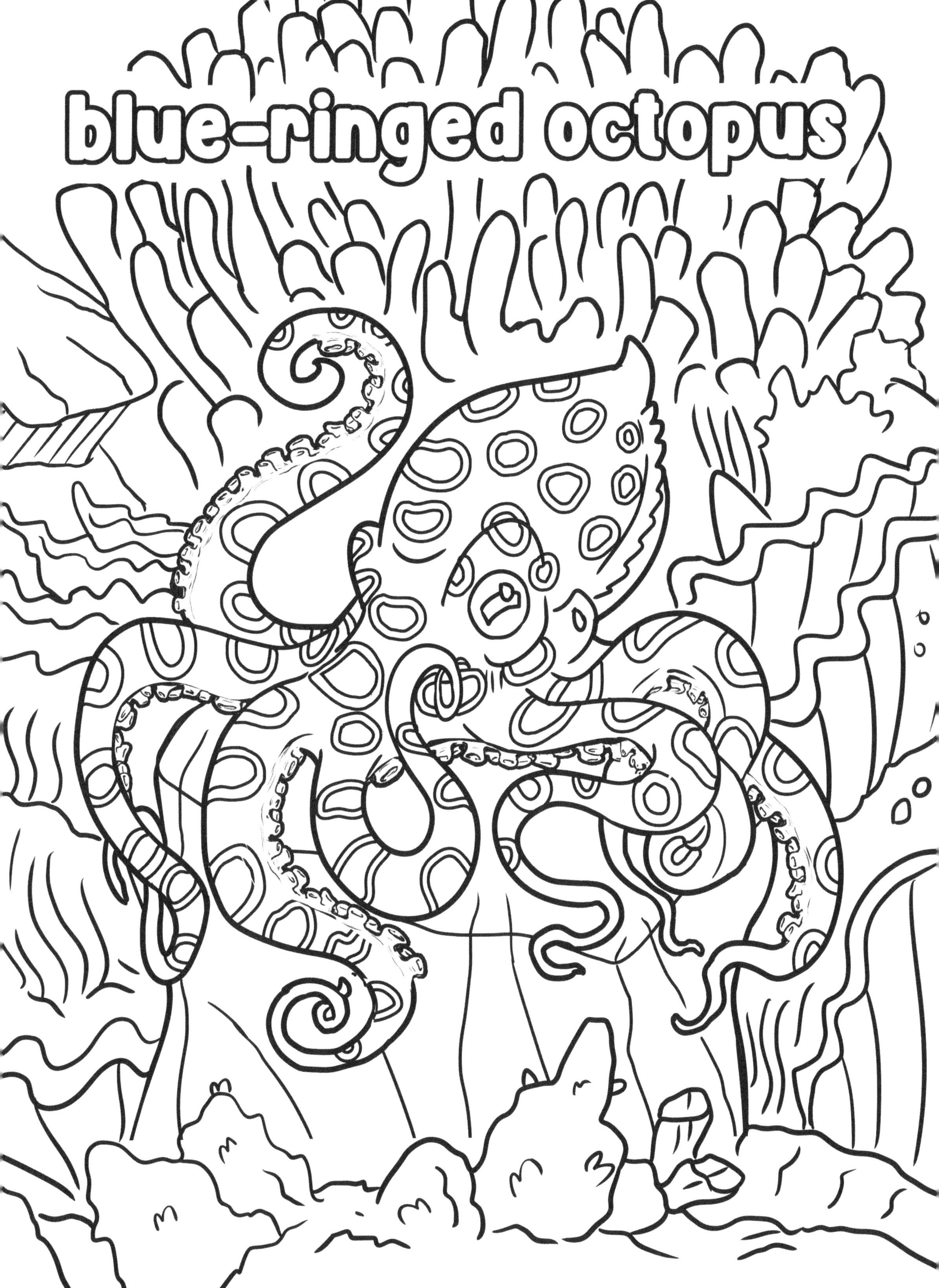
blue-ringed octopus

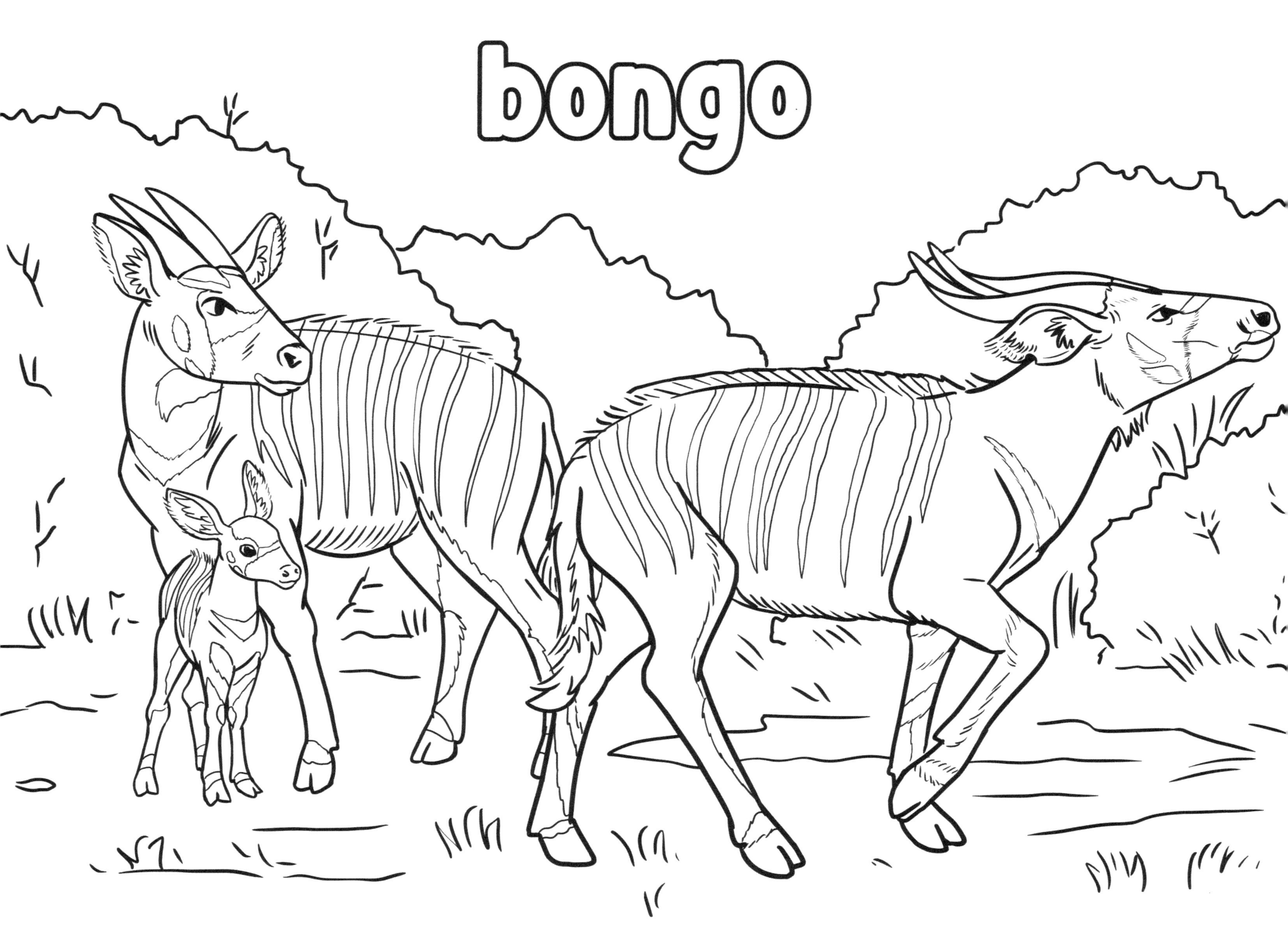
bongo

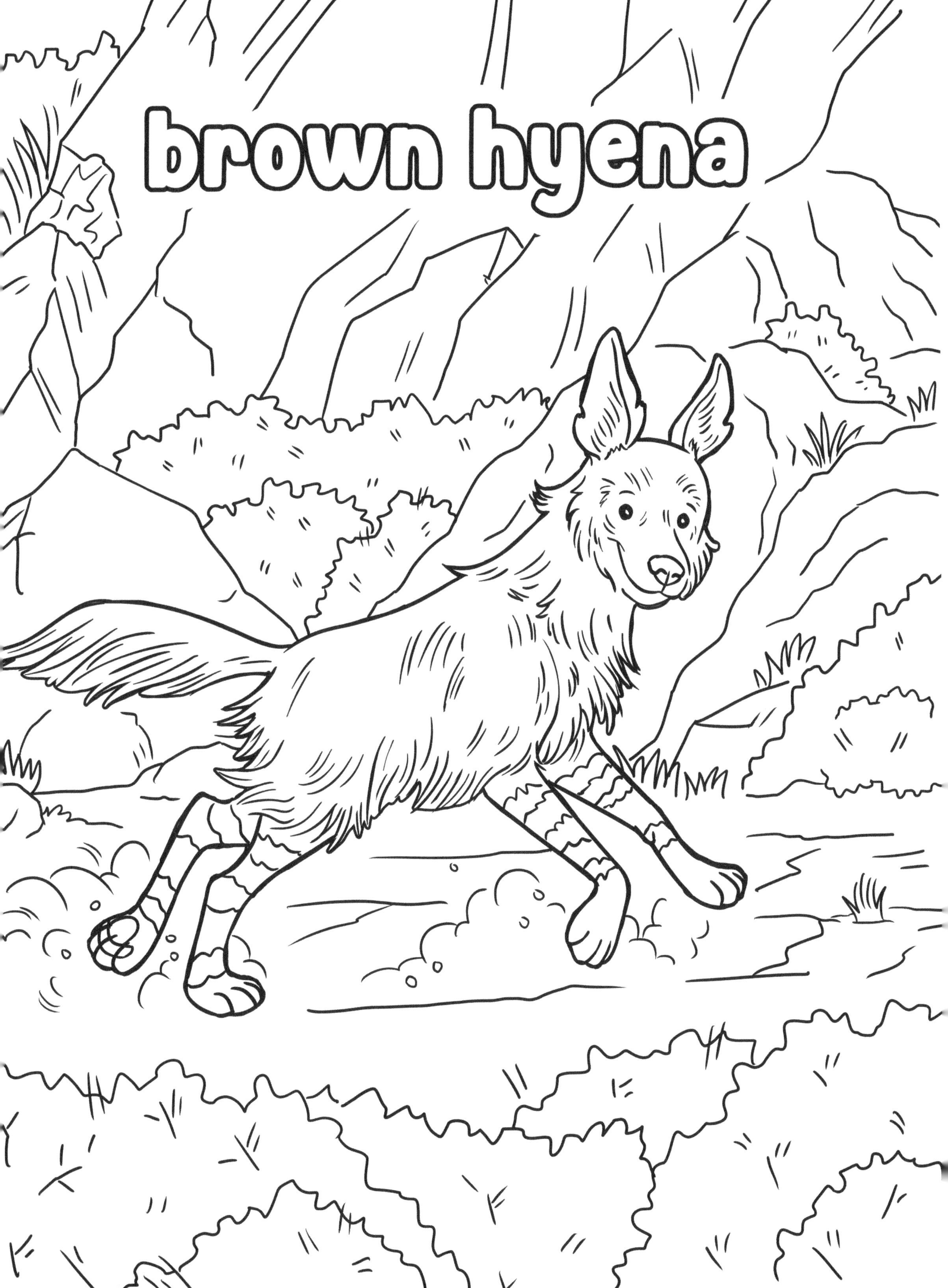
brown hyena

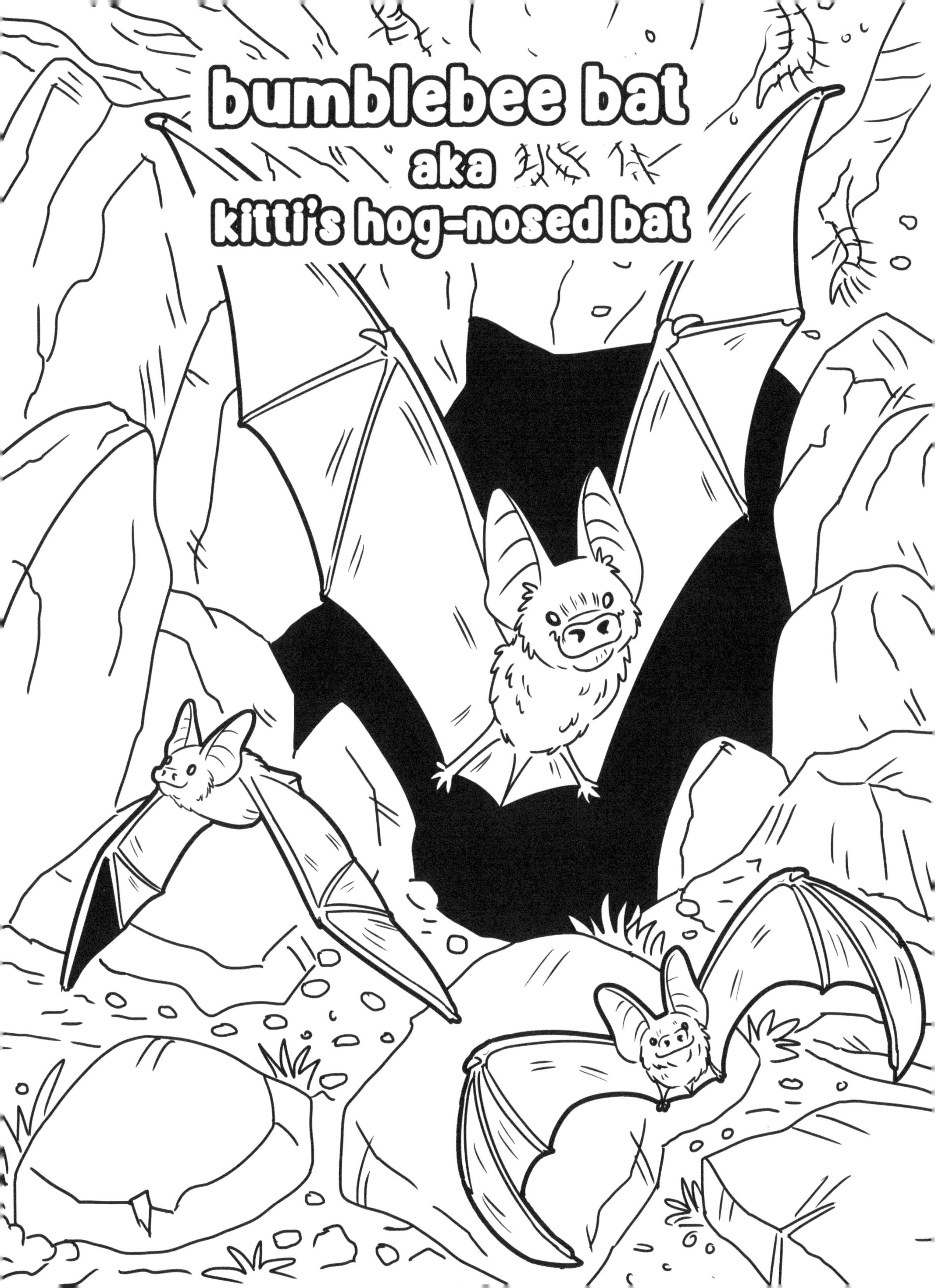
bumblebee bat
aka
kitti's hog-nosed bat

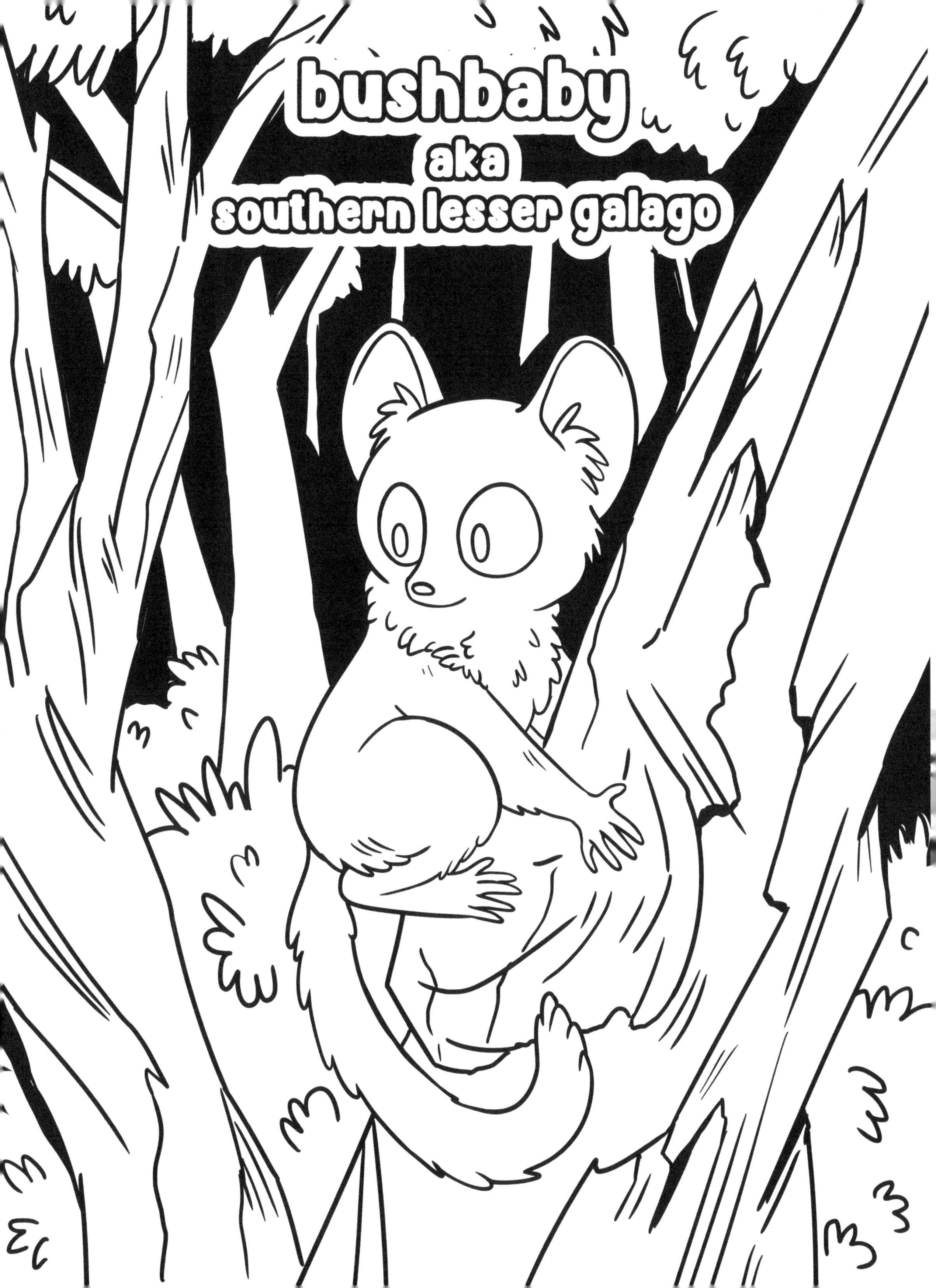
bushbaby
aka
southern lesser galago

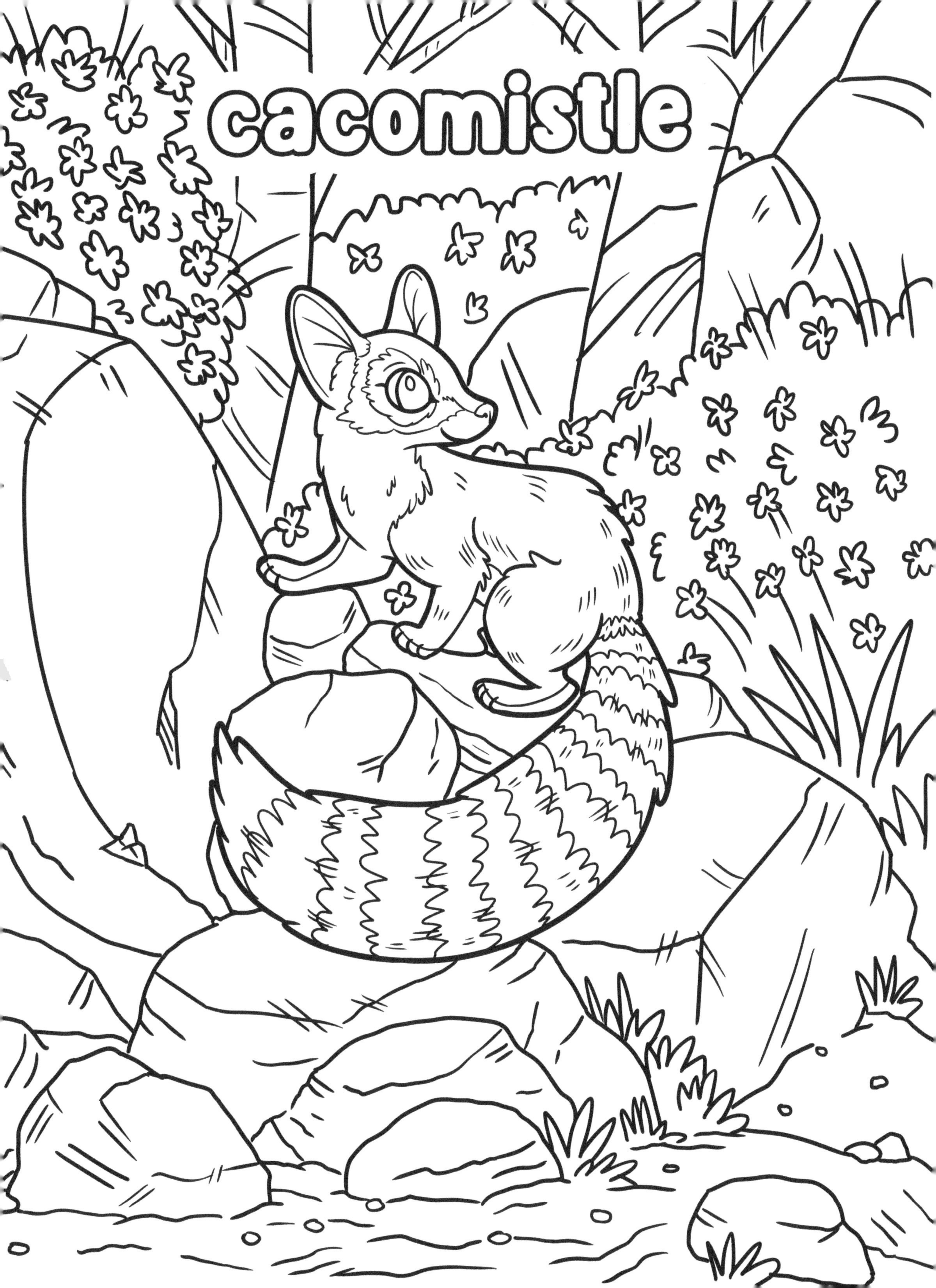
cacomistle

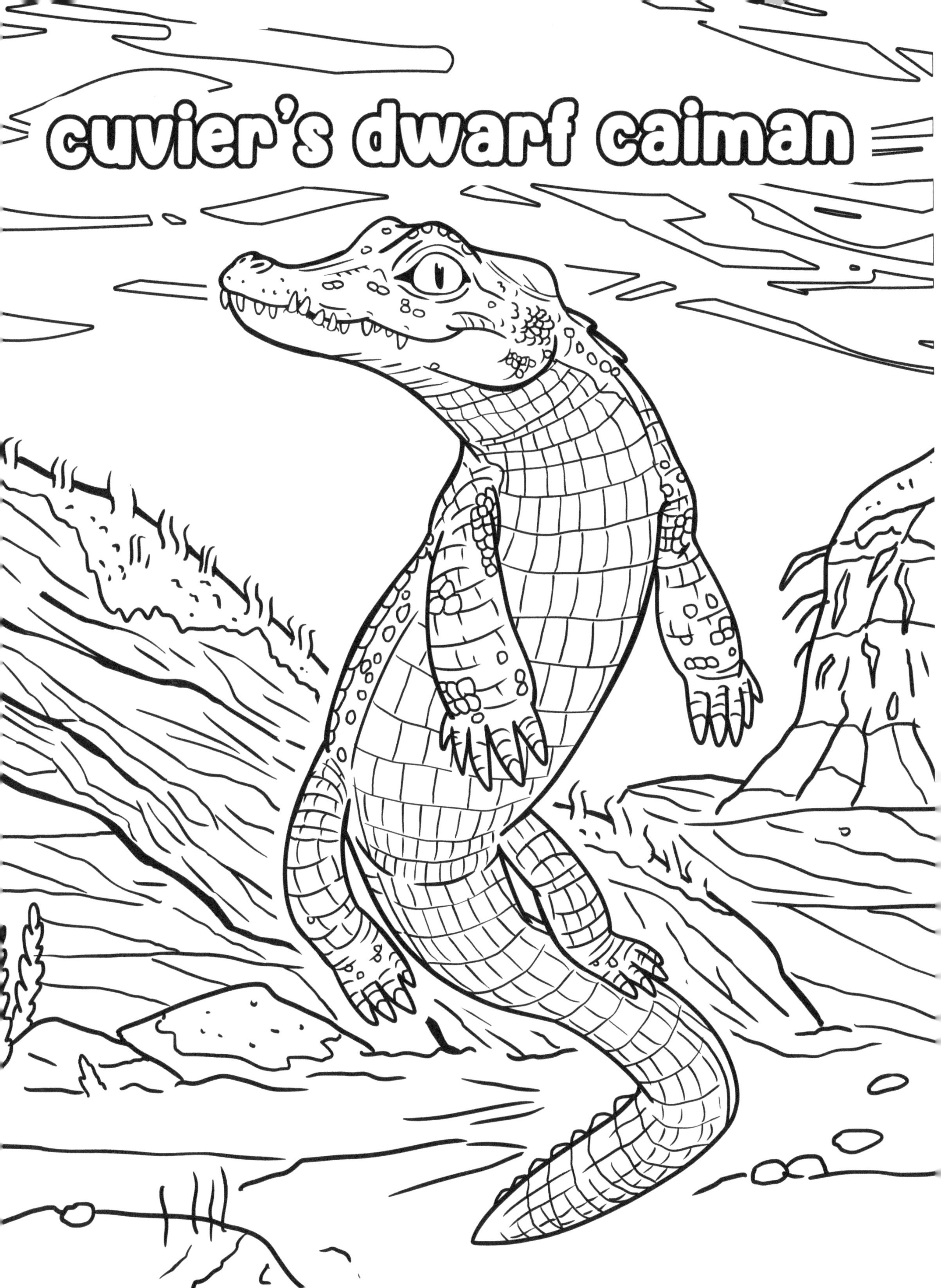
cuvier's dwarf caiman

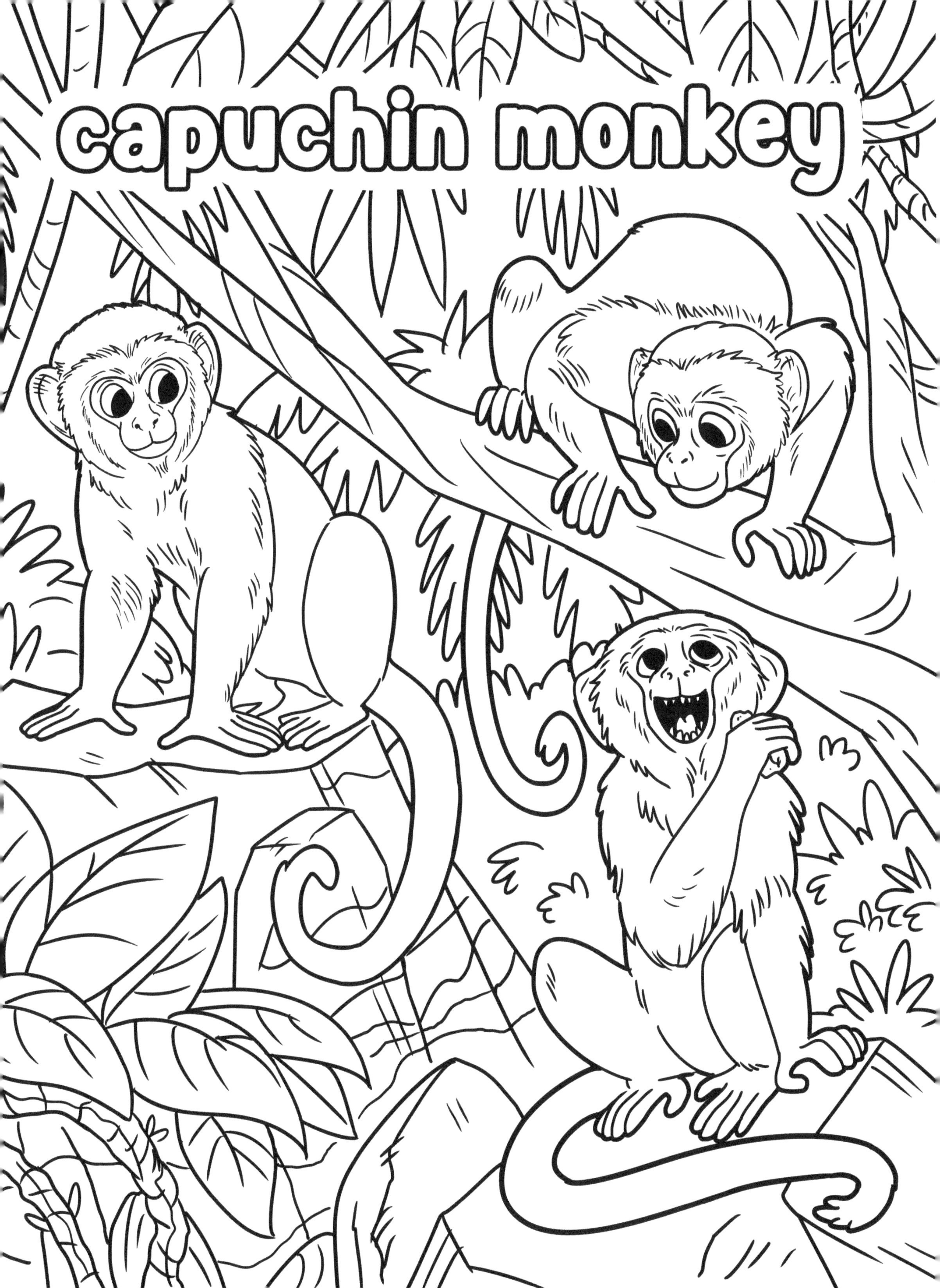
capuchin monkey

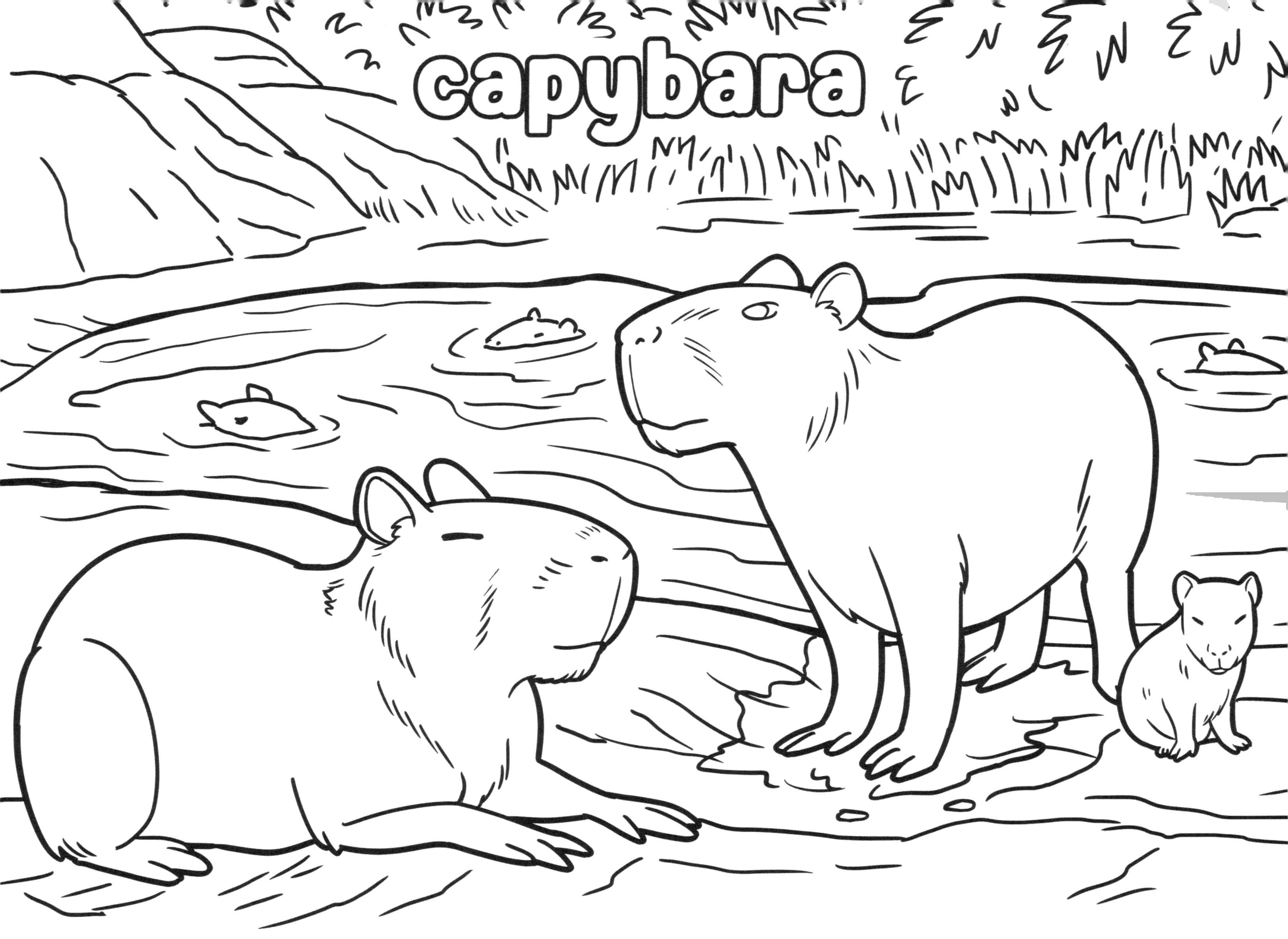
capybara

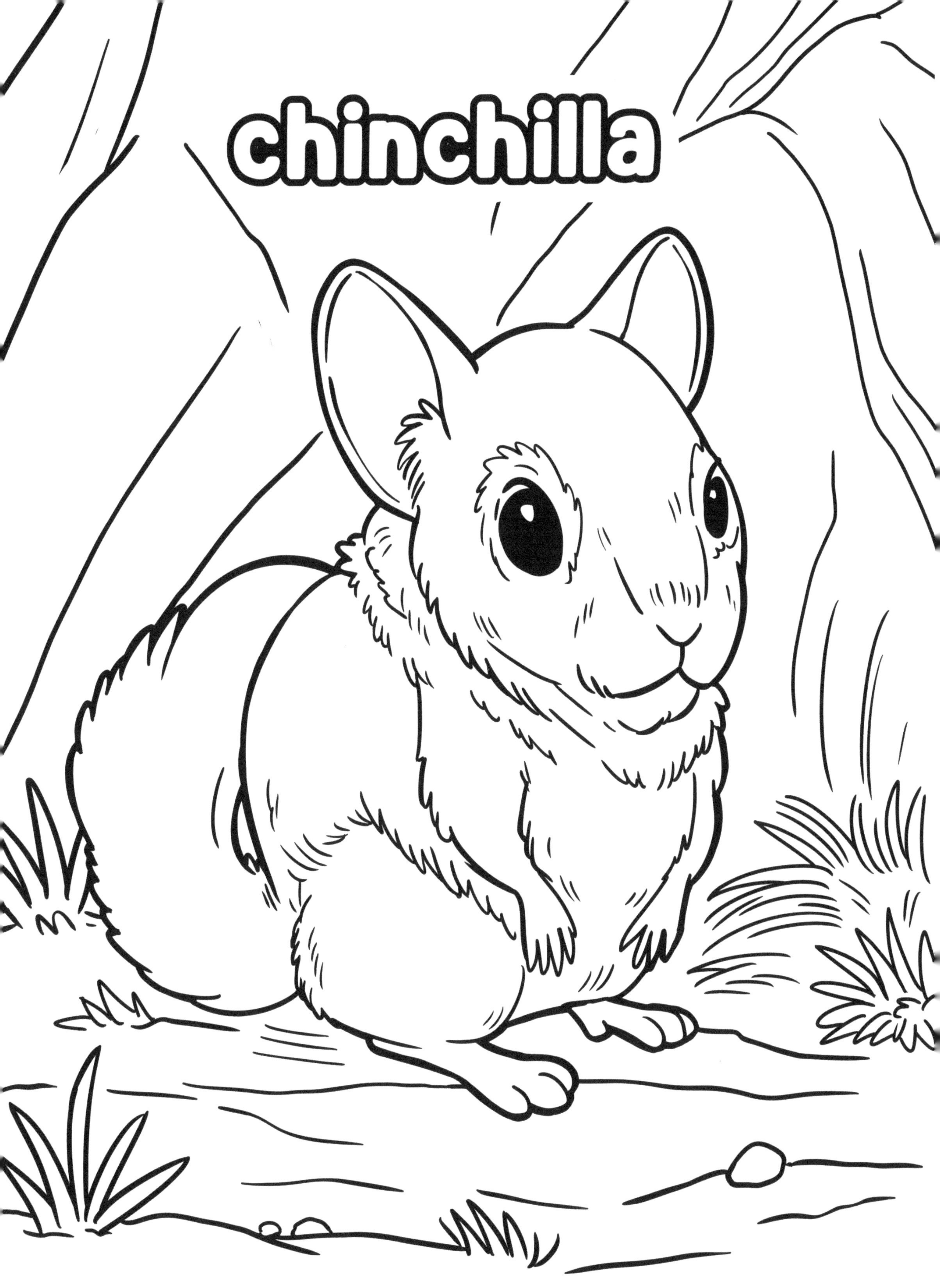
chinchilla

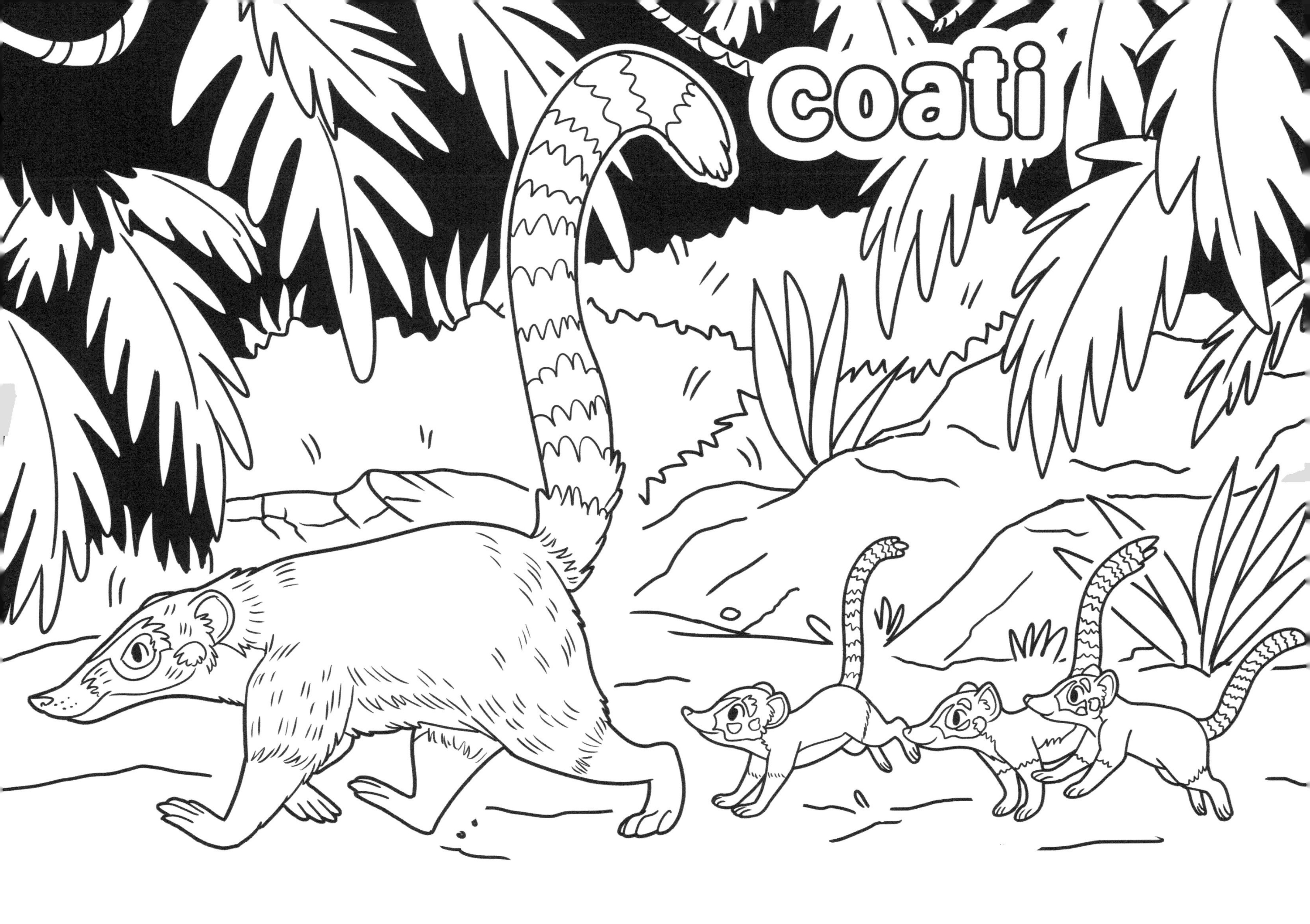
coati

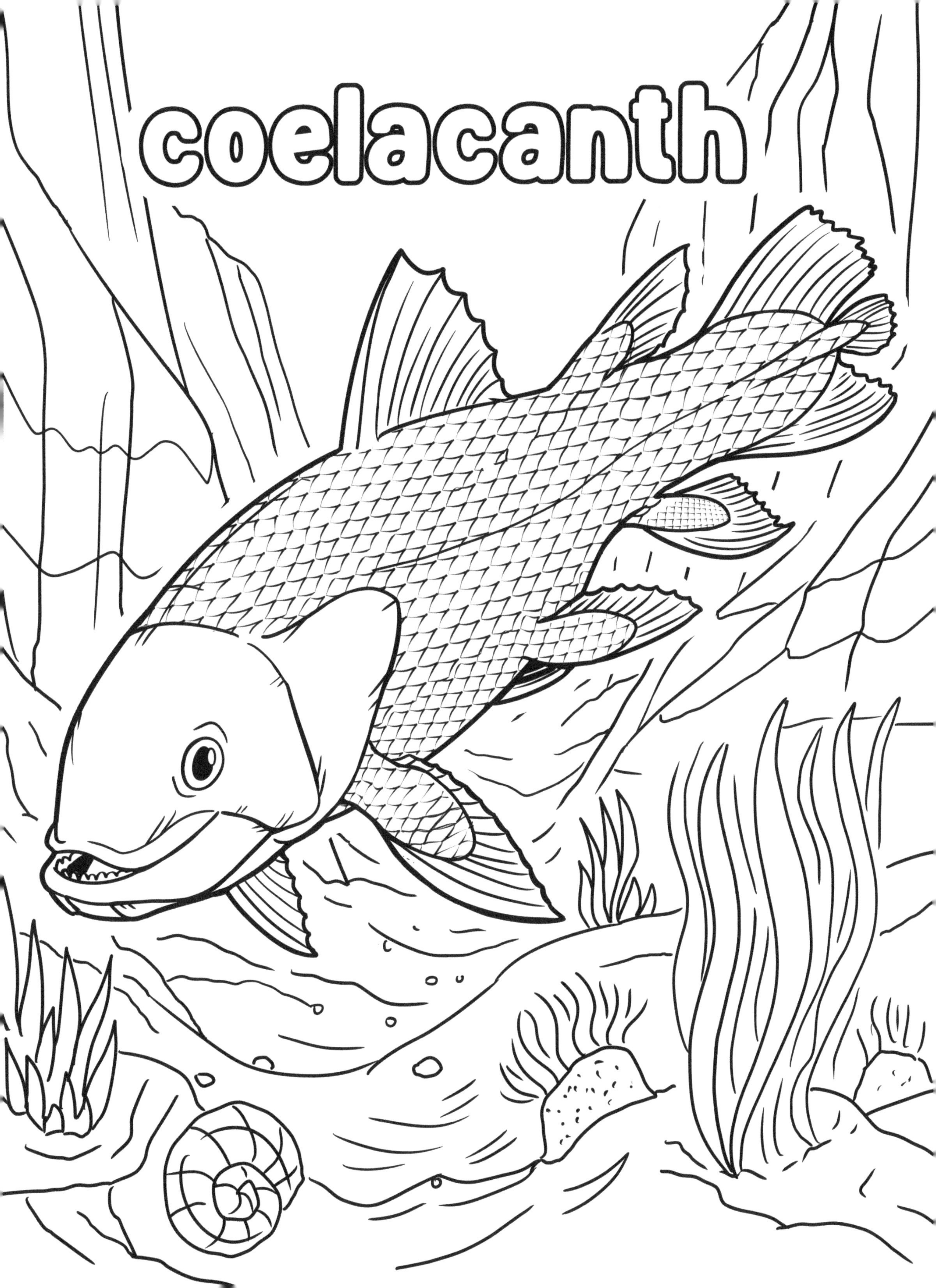
coelacanth

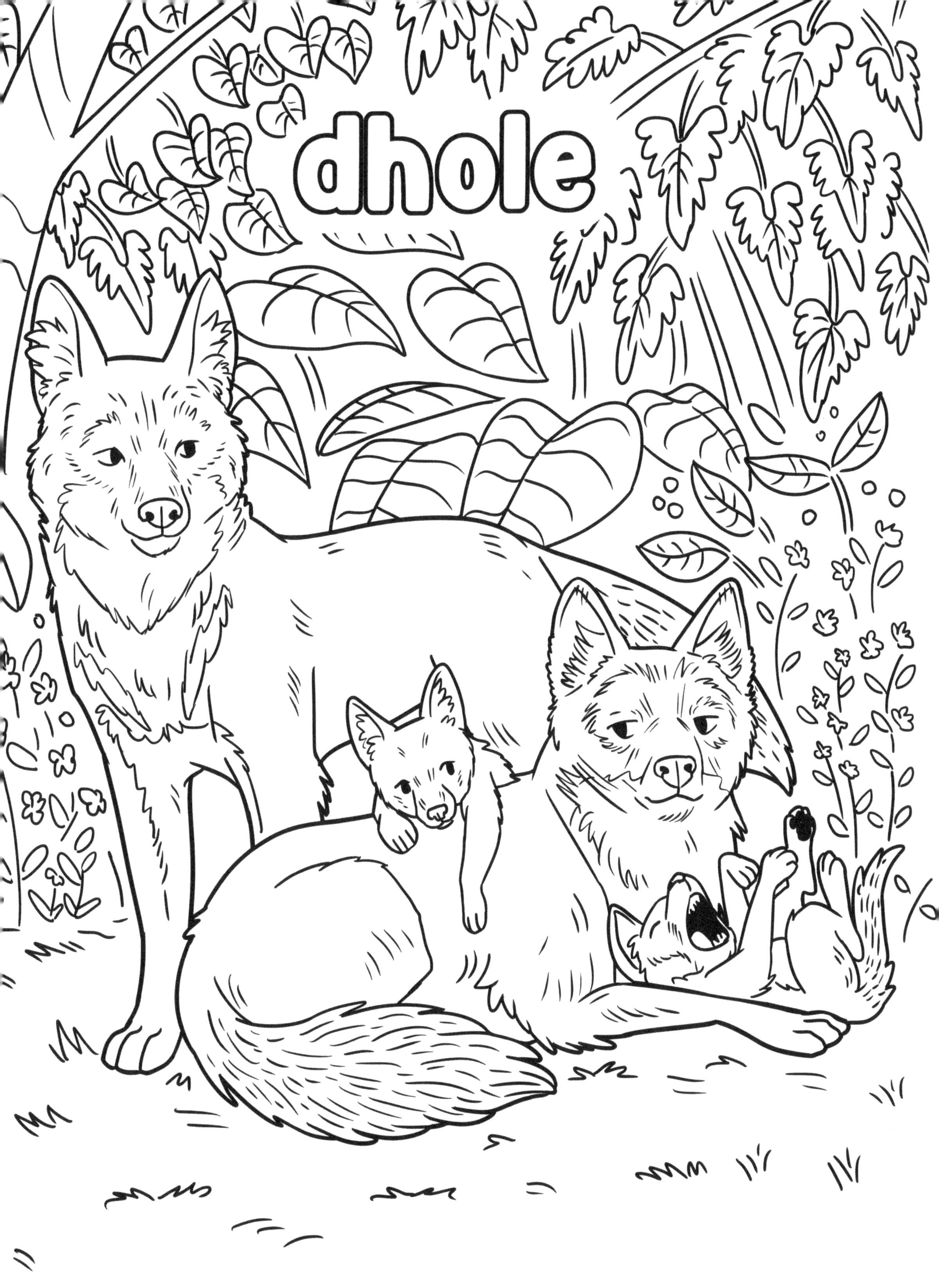
dhole

dik-dik

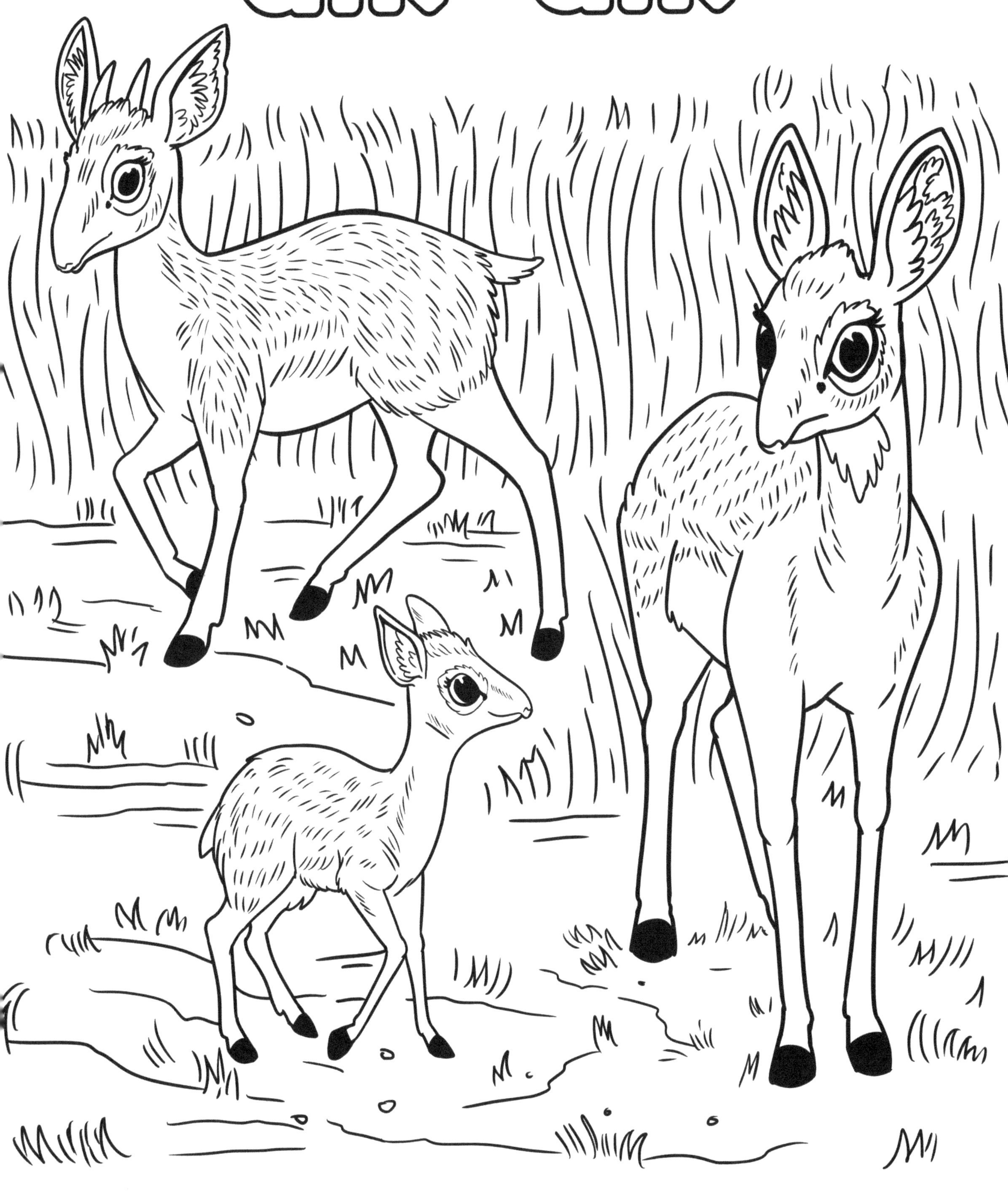

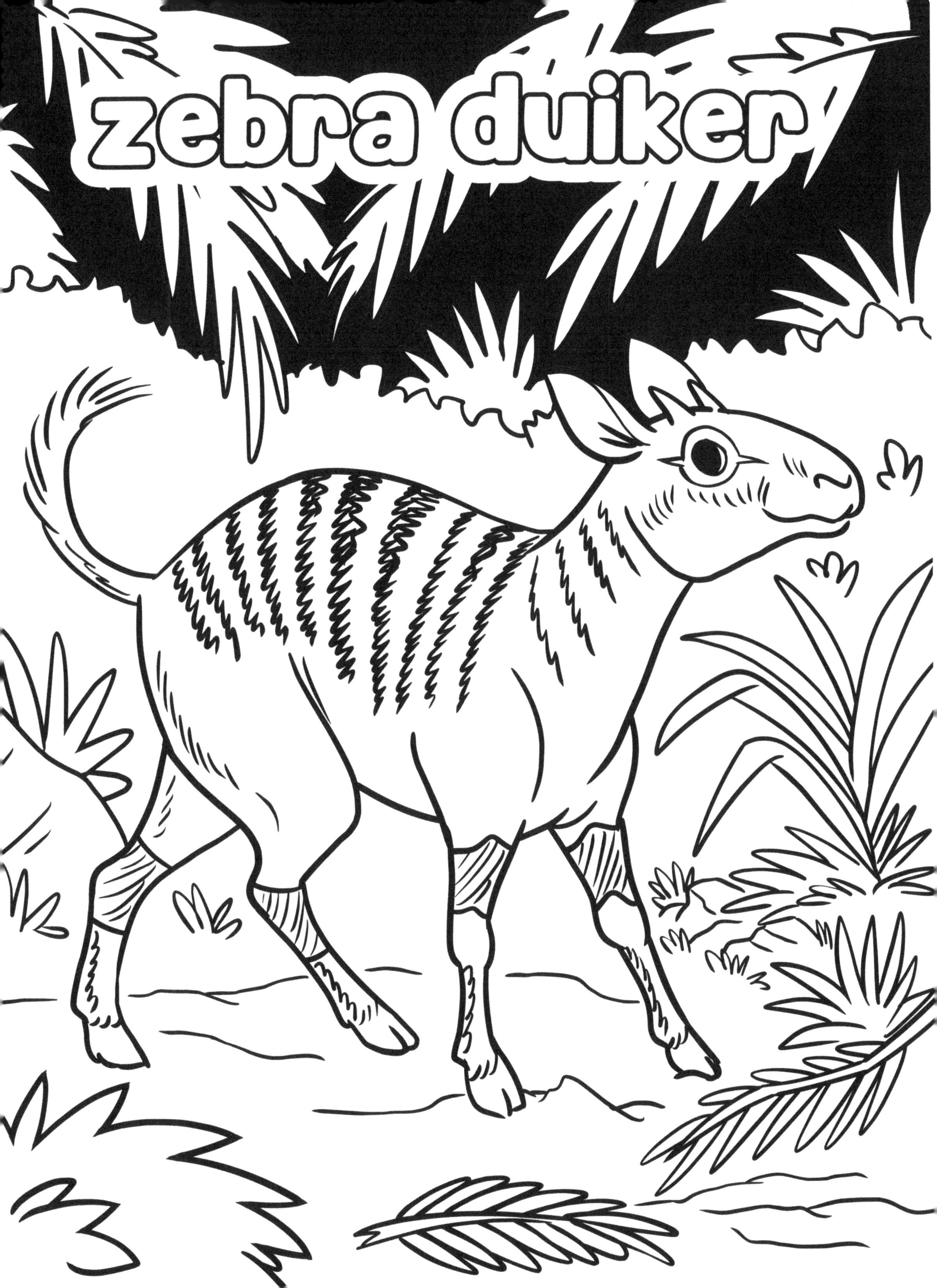
zebra duiker

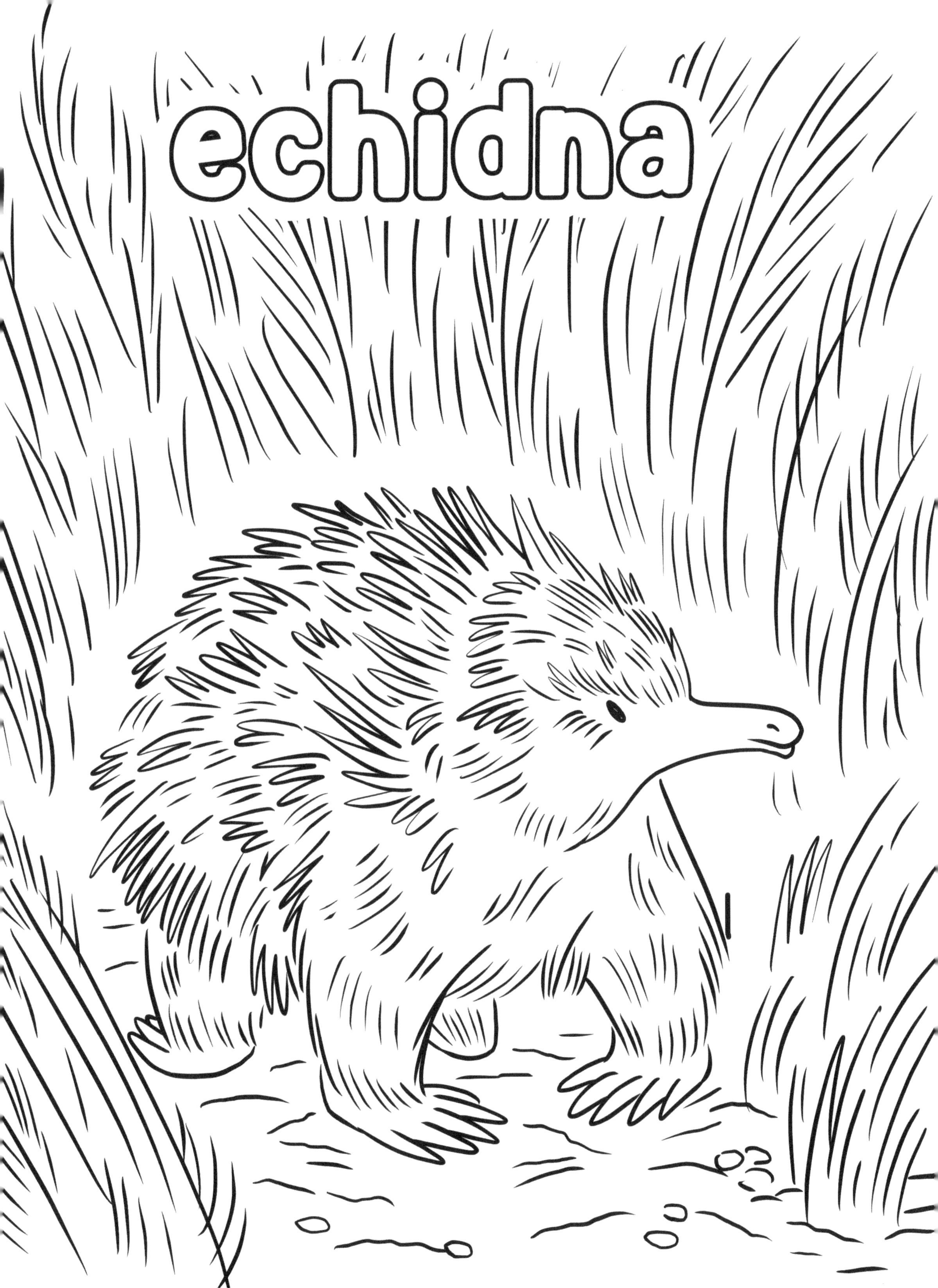
echidna

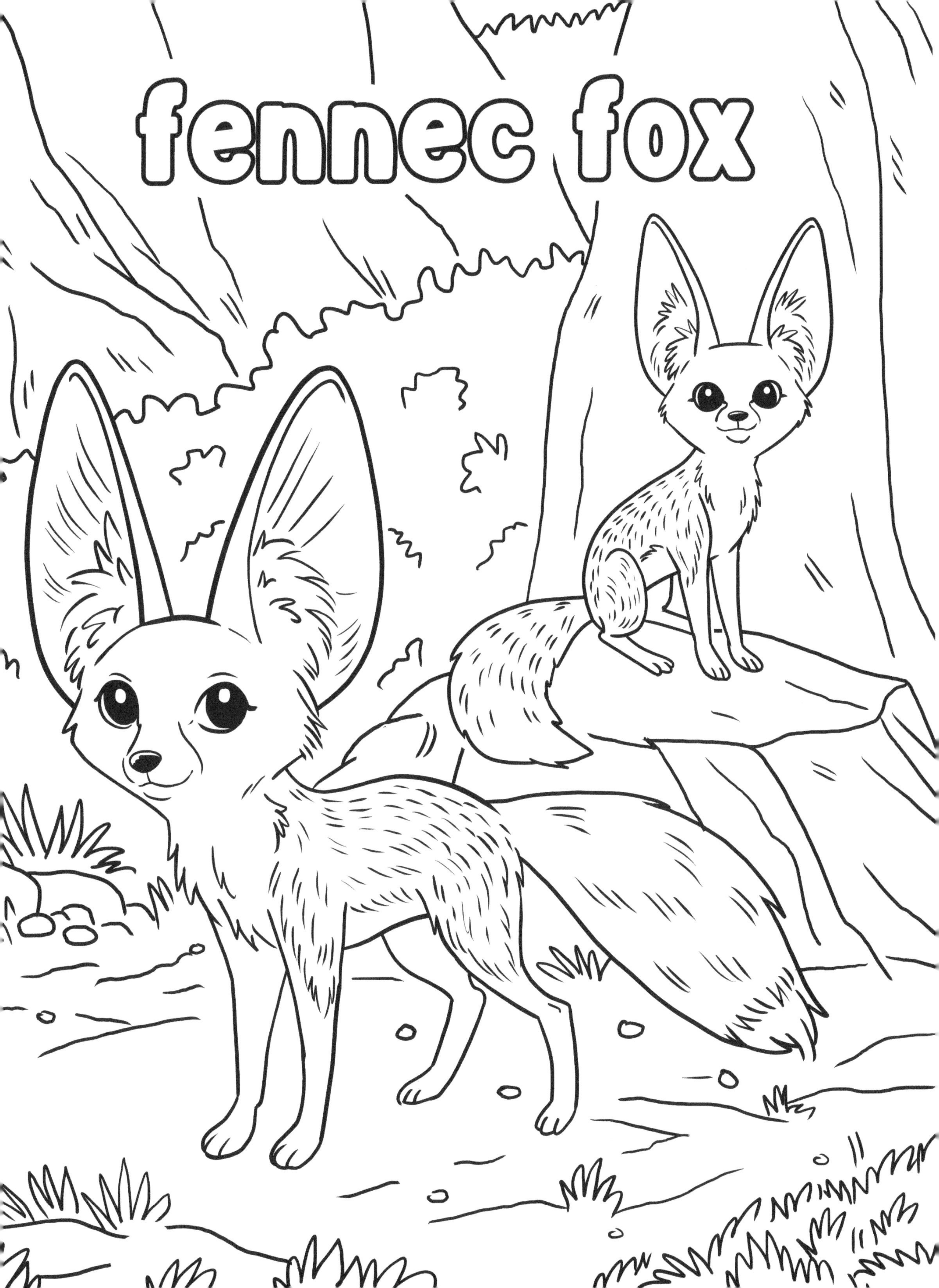
fennec fox

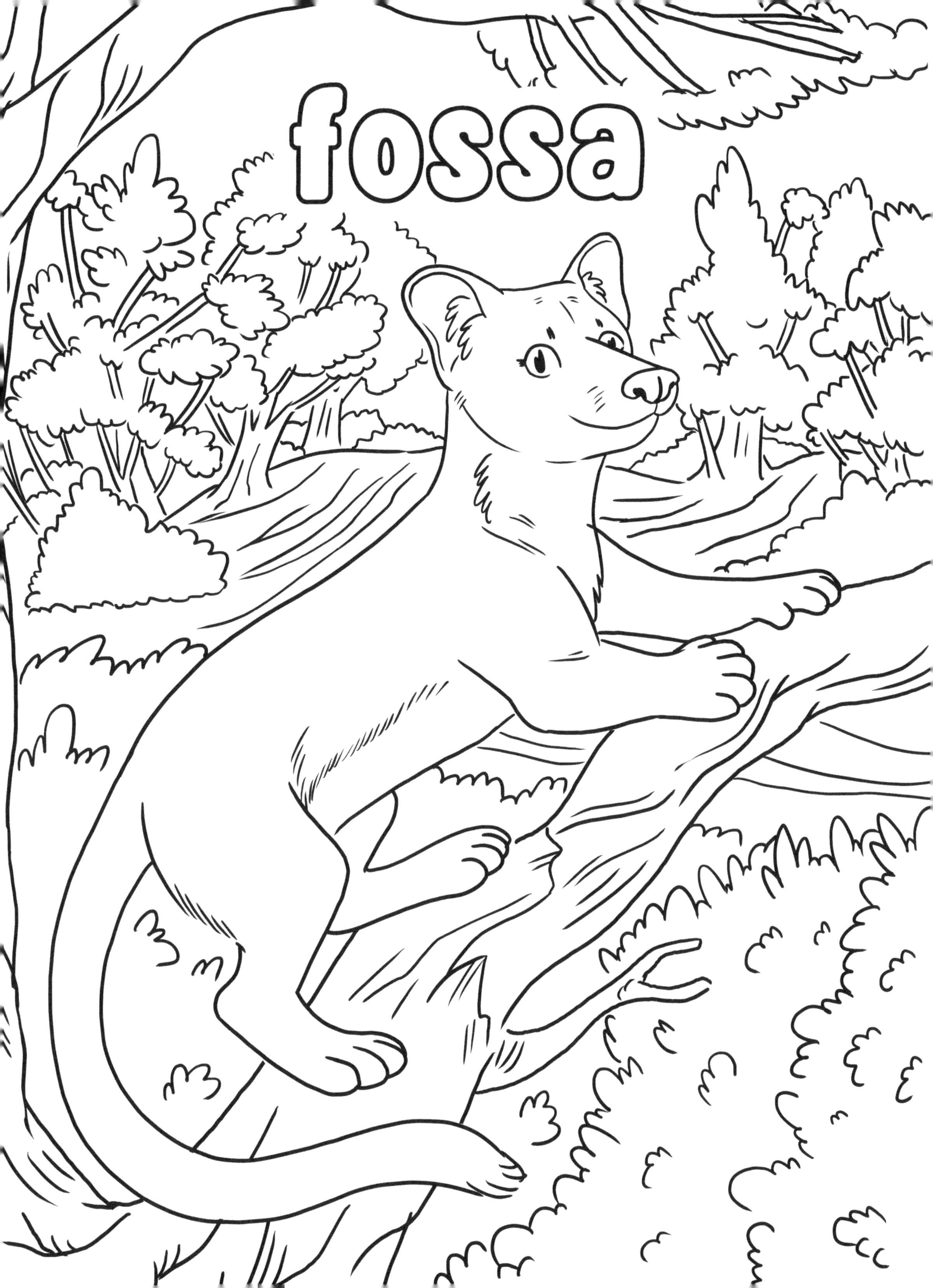
fossa

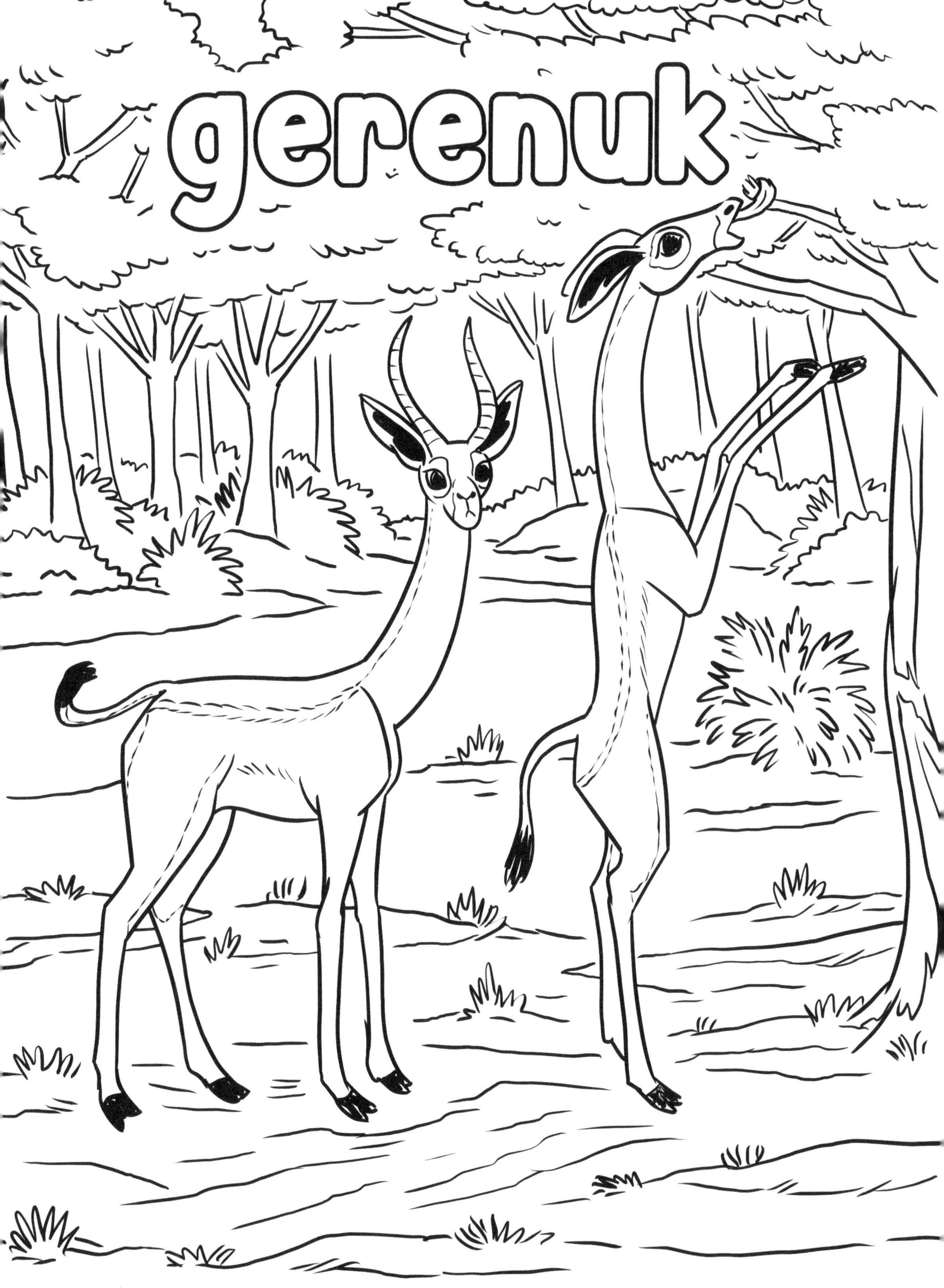
gerenuk

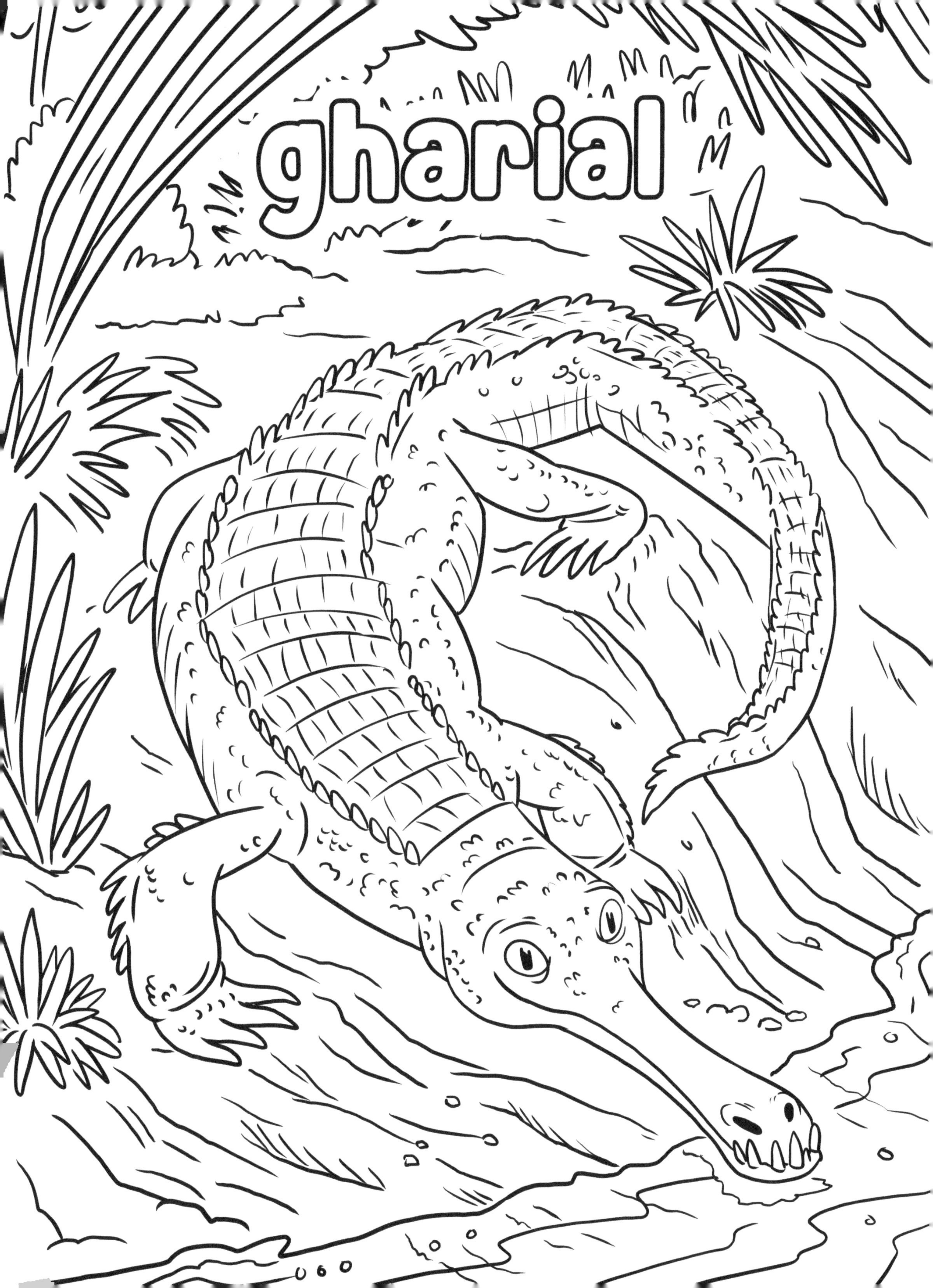
gharial

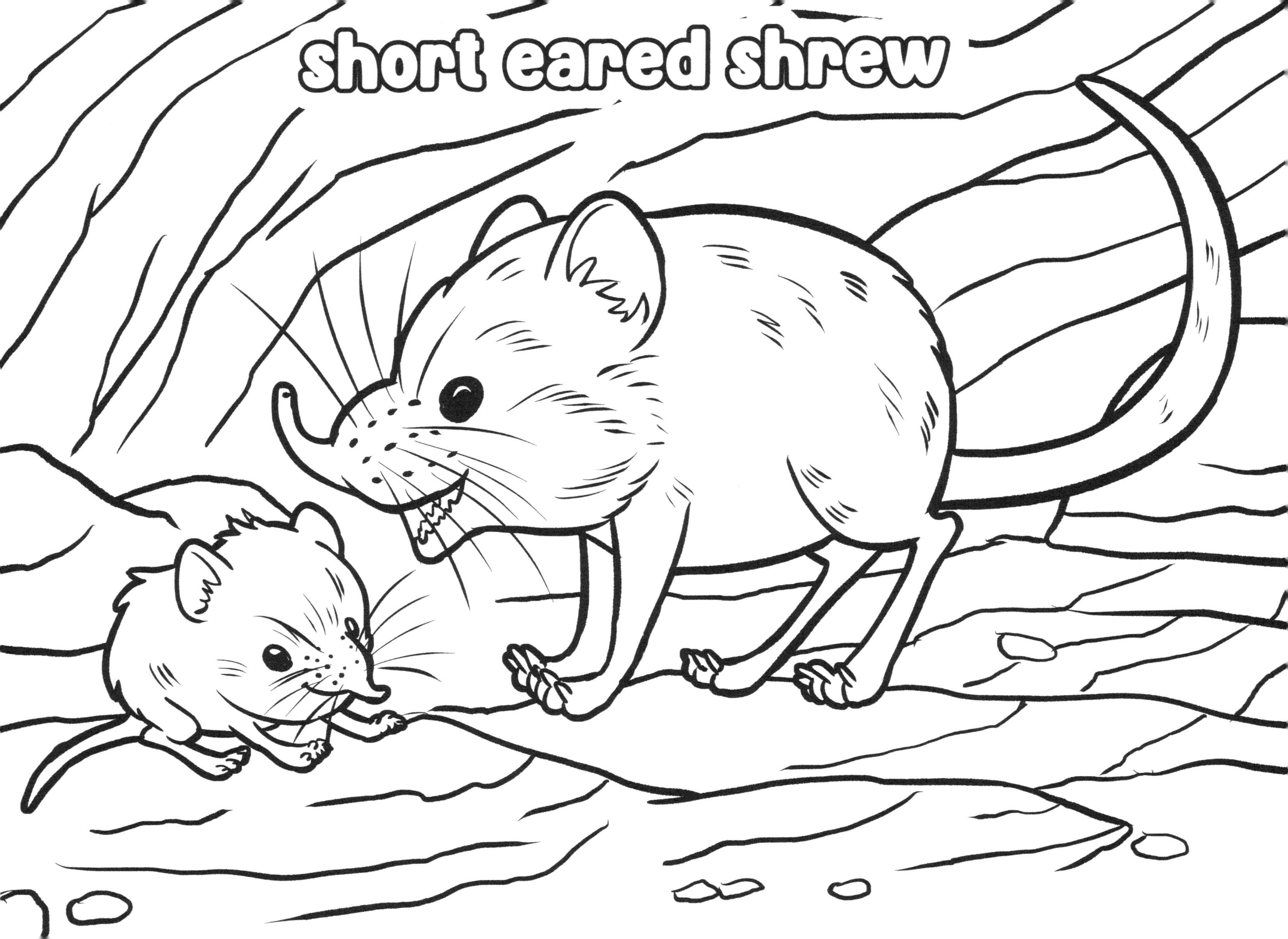
short eared shrew

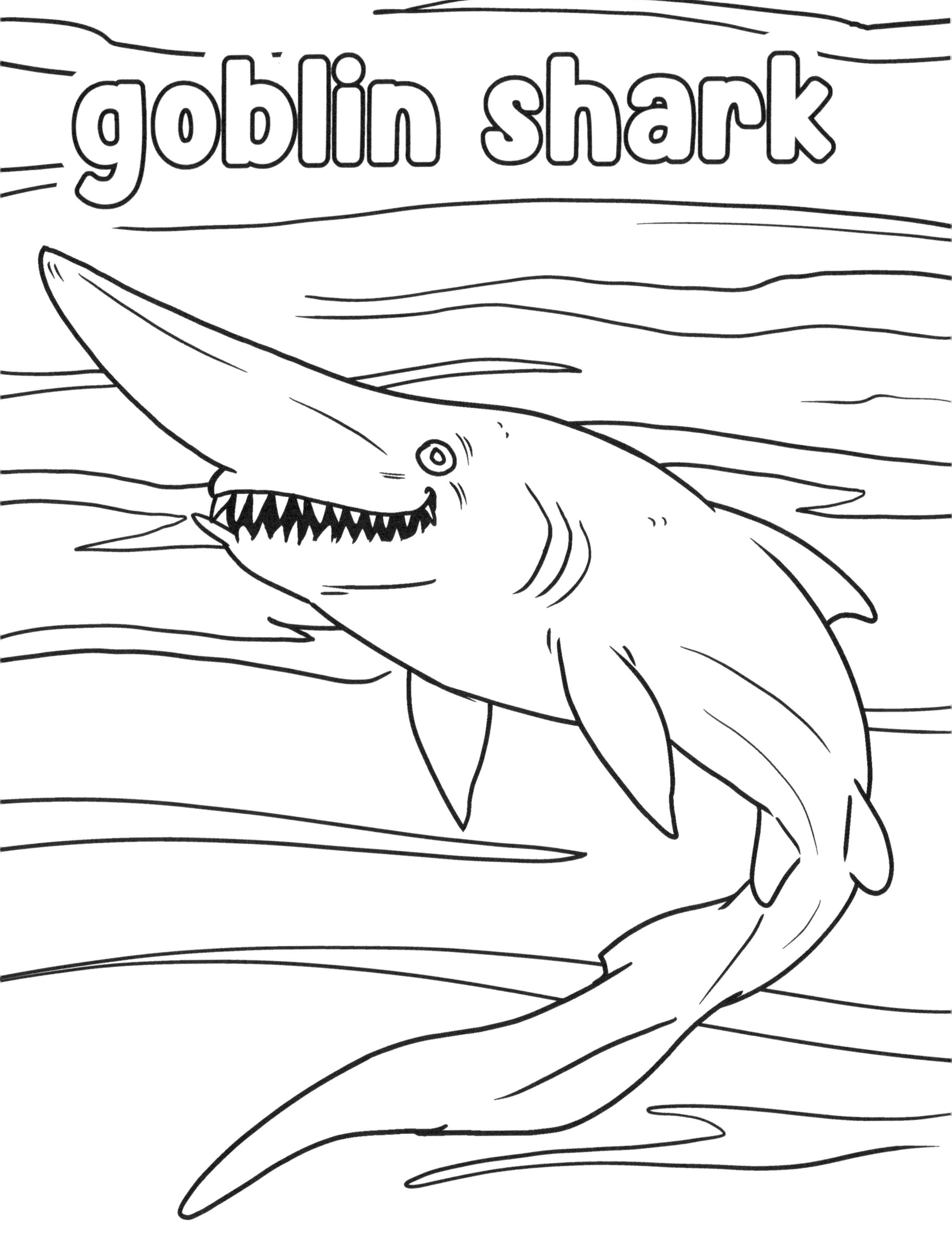
goblin shark

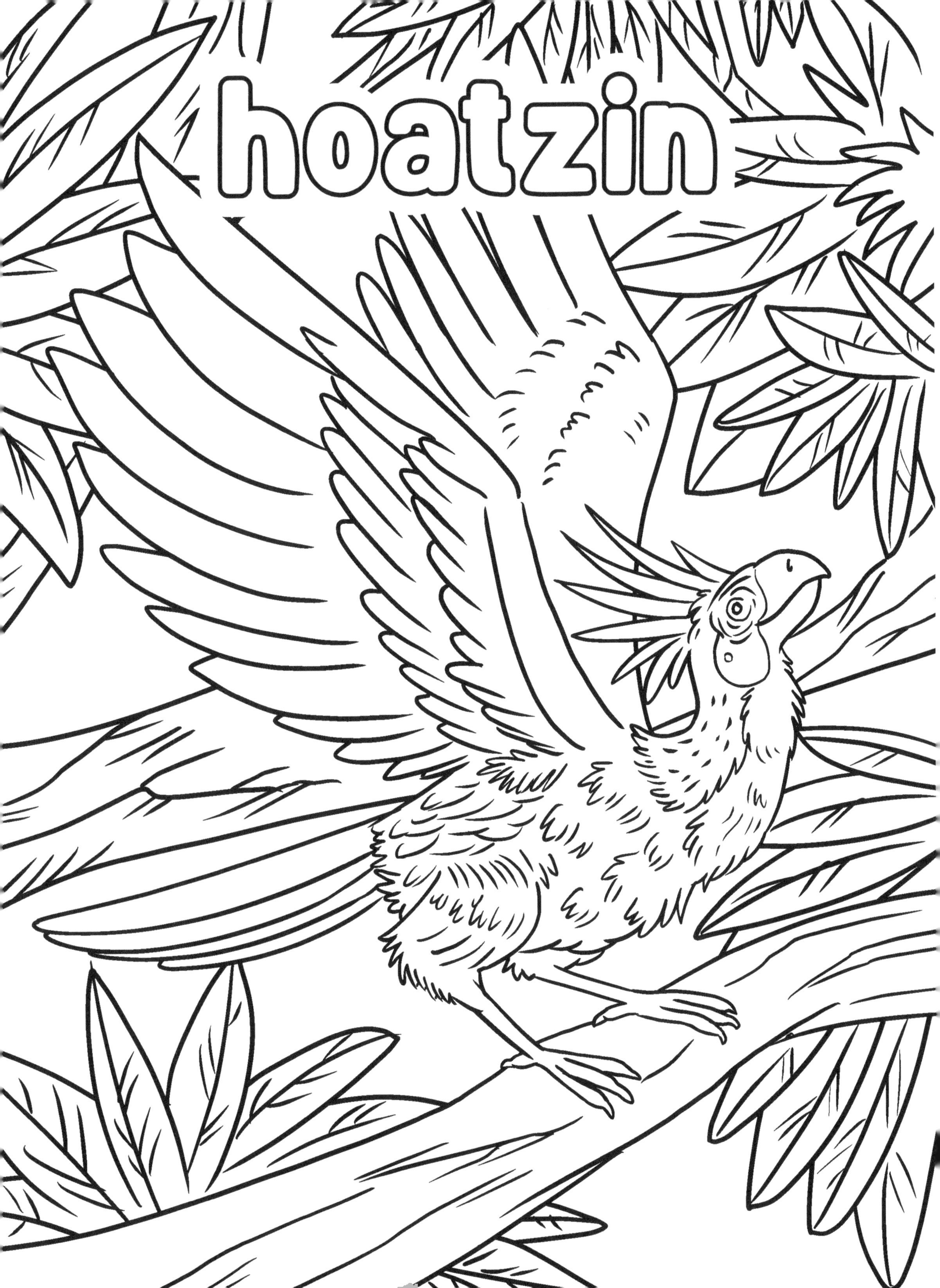
hoatzin

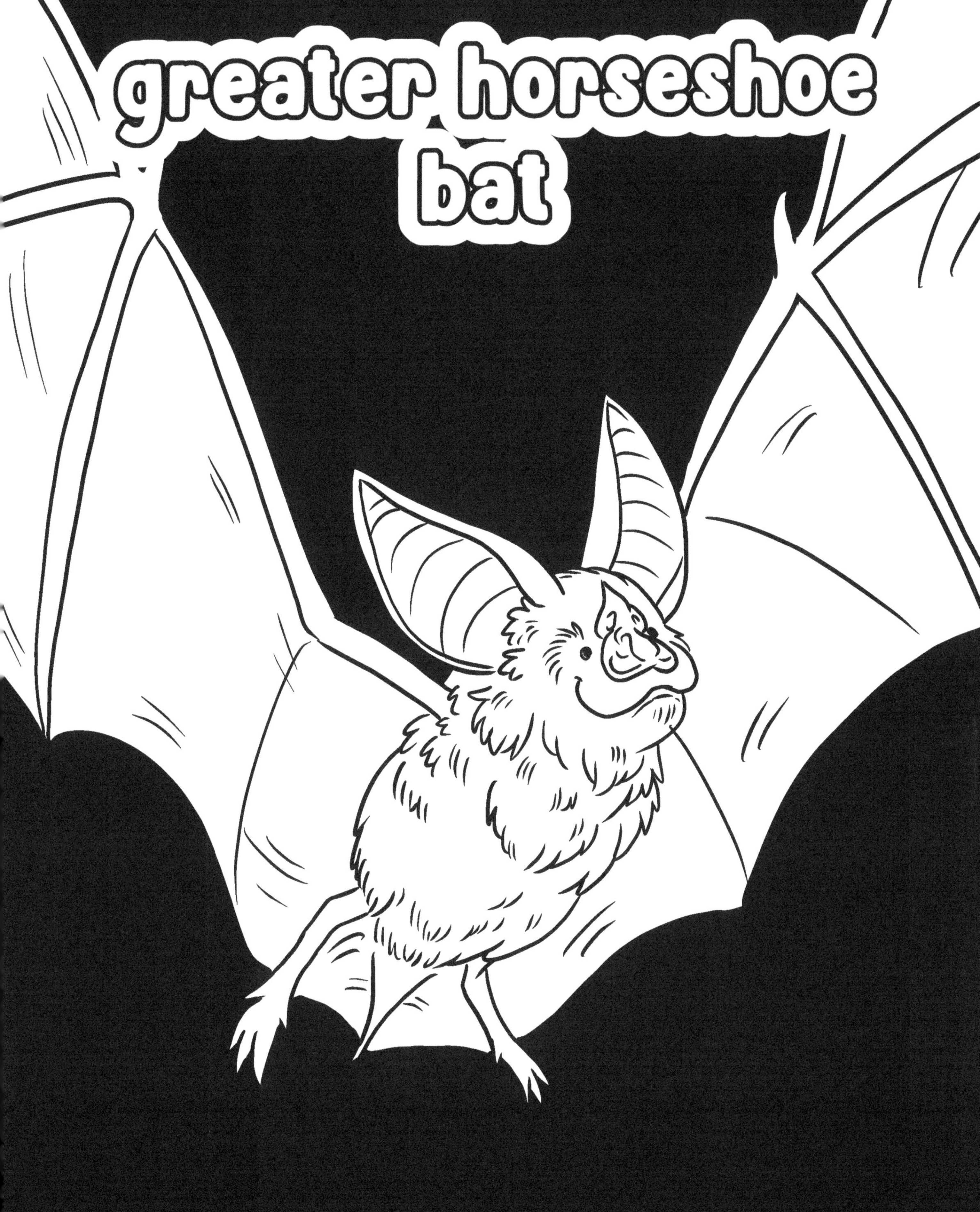
greater horseshoe
bat

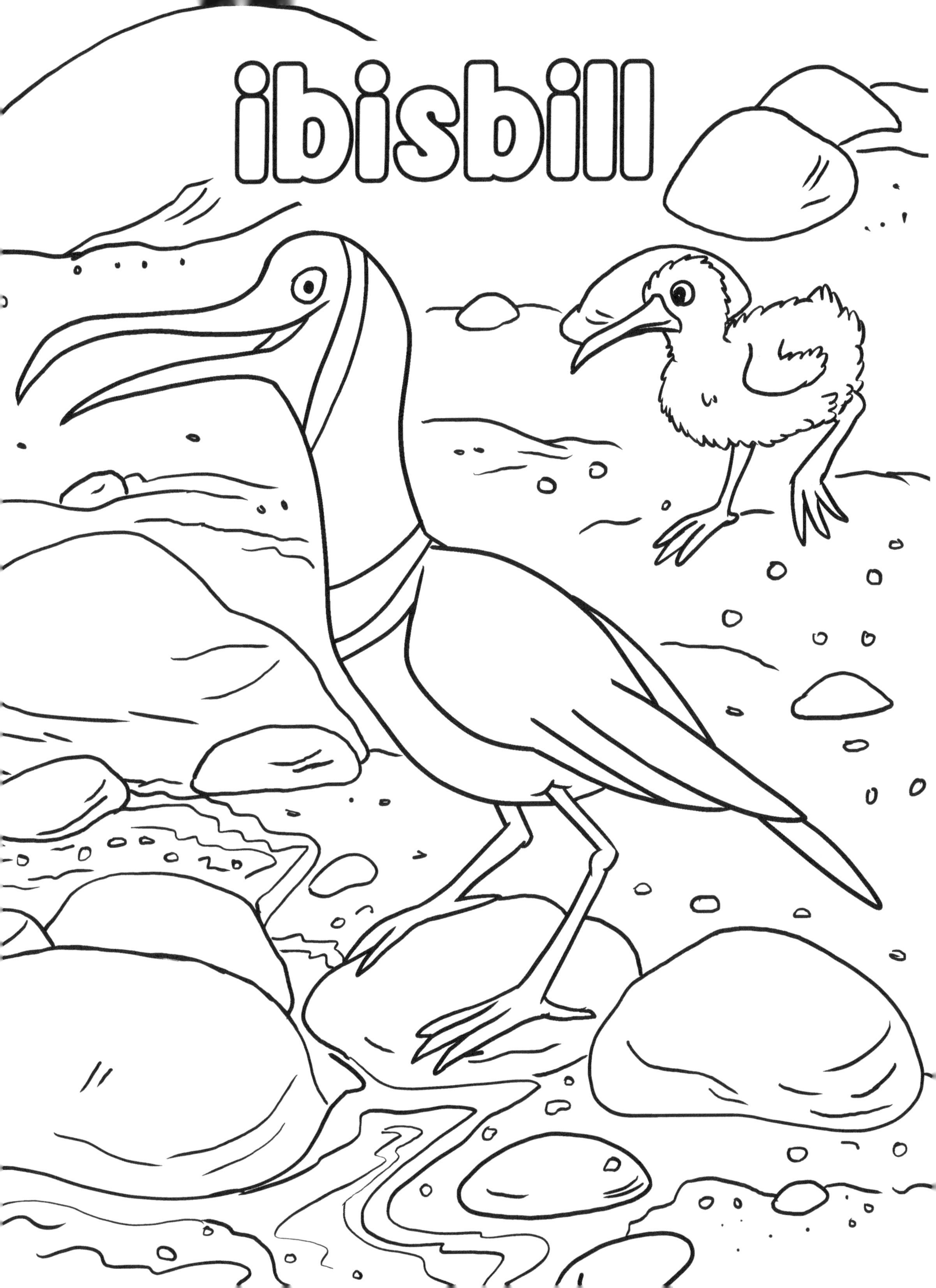
ibisbill

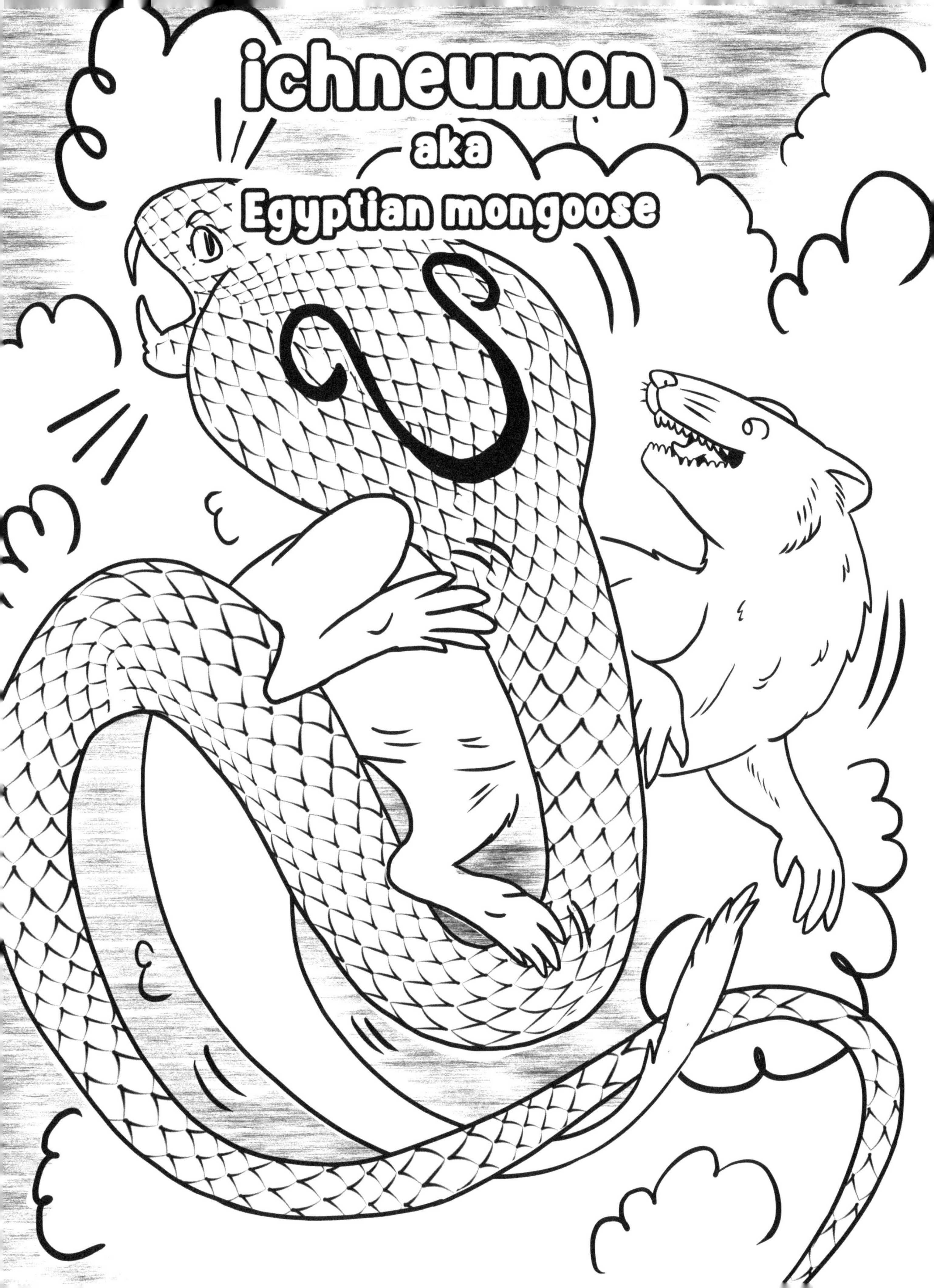
ichneumon
aka
Egyptian mongoose

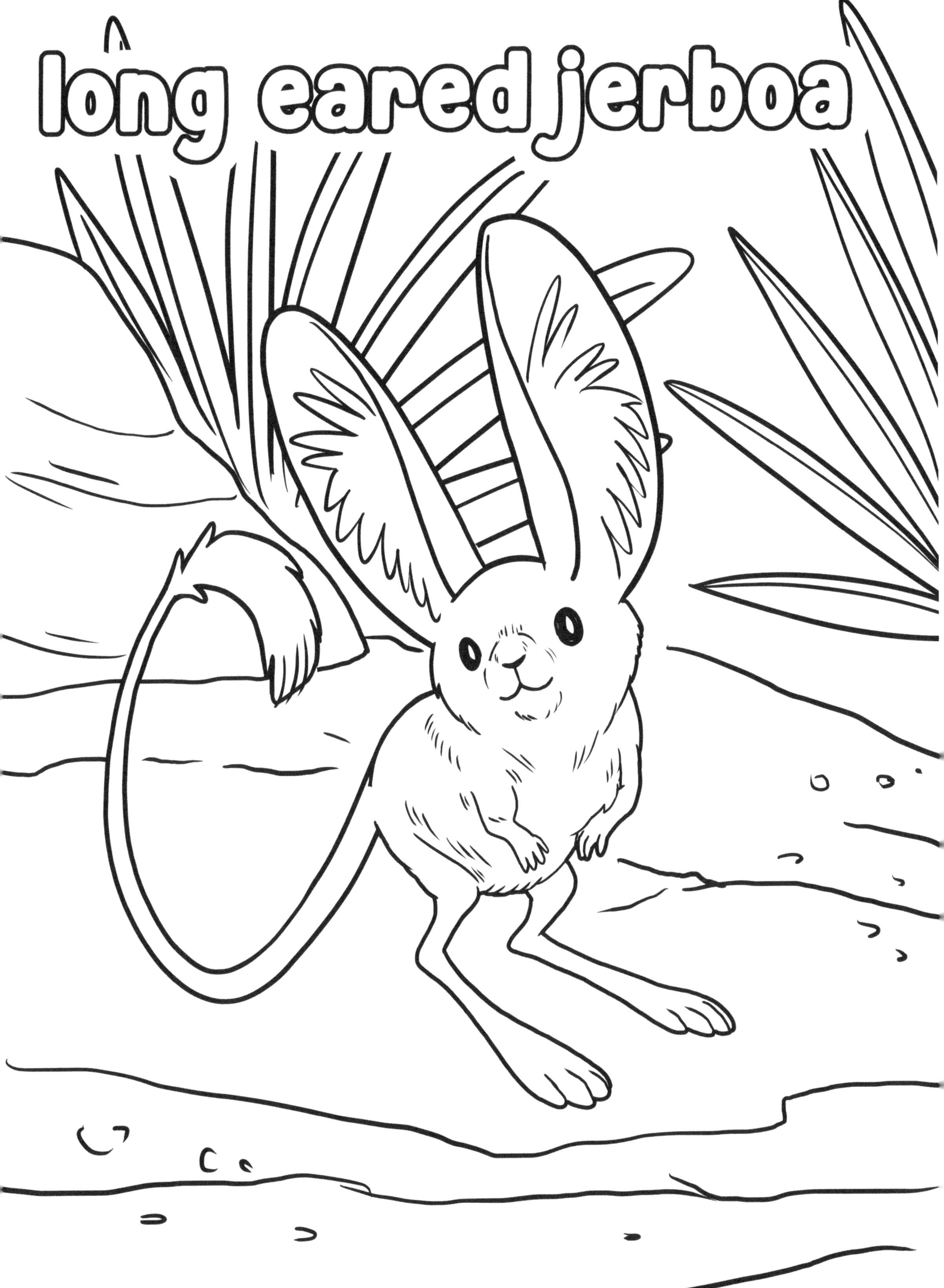
long eared jerboa

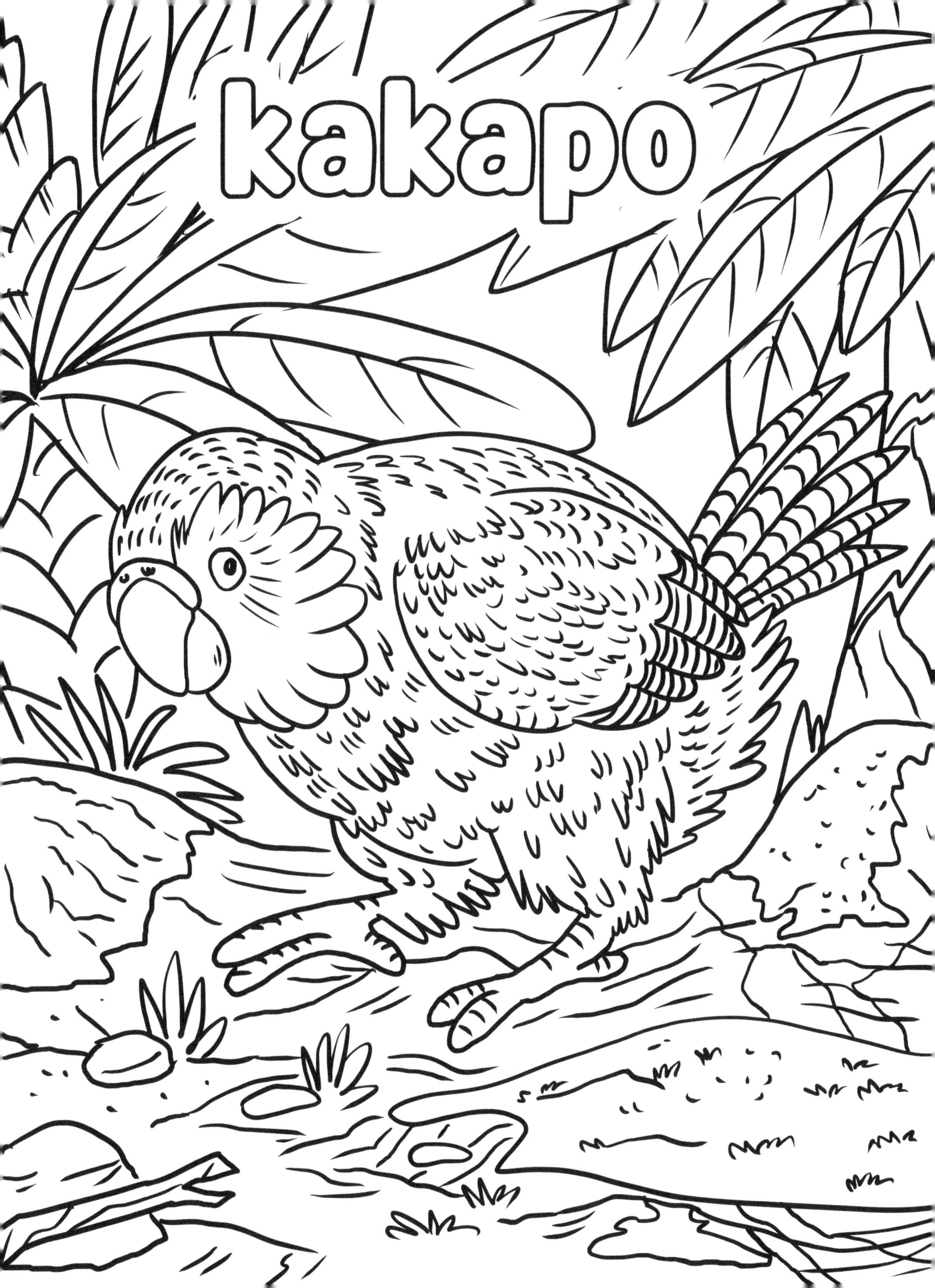
kakapo

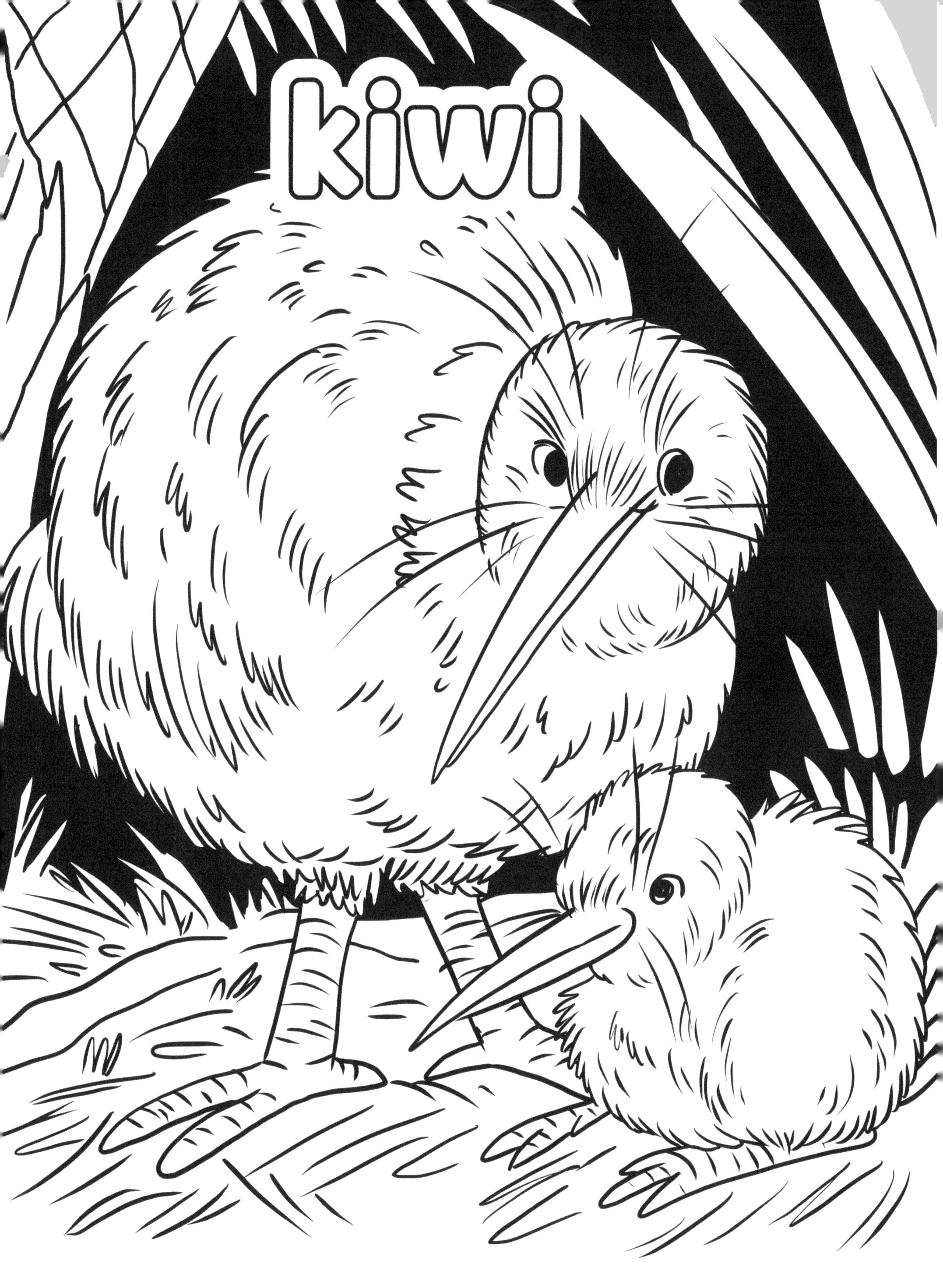
kiwi

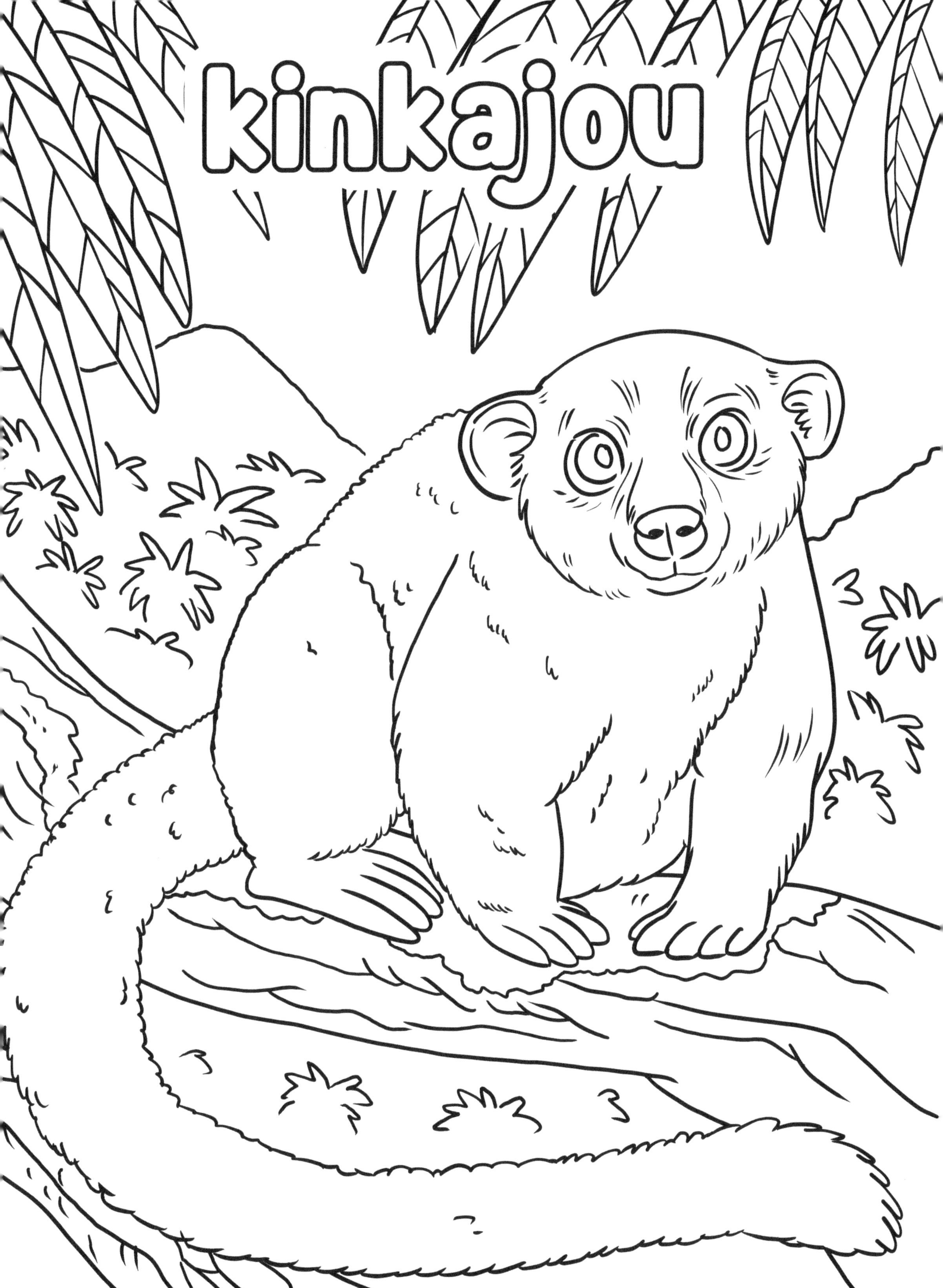
kinkajou

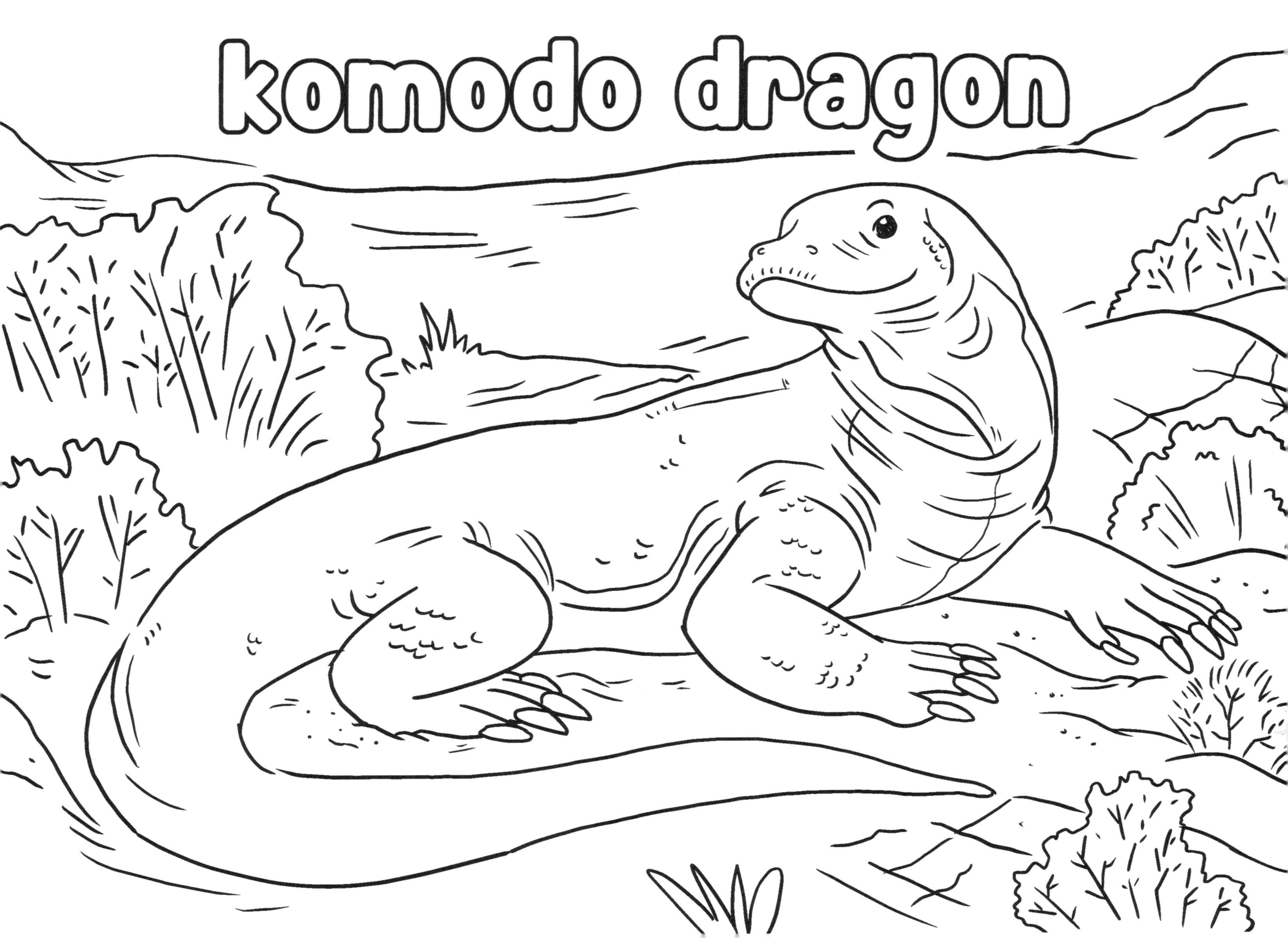
komodo dragon

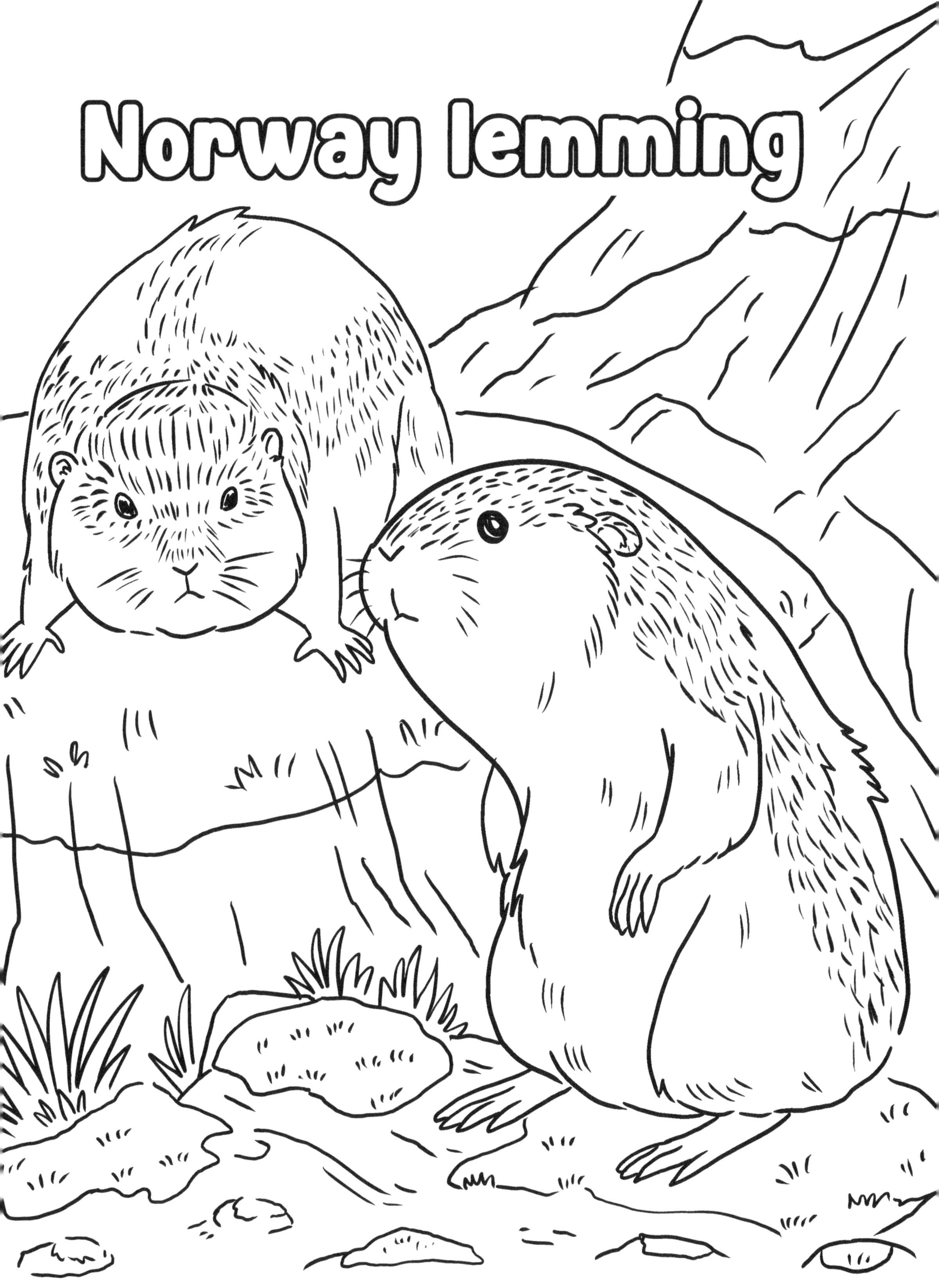
Norway lemming

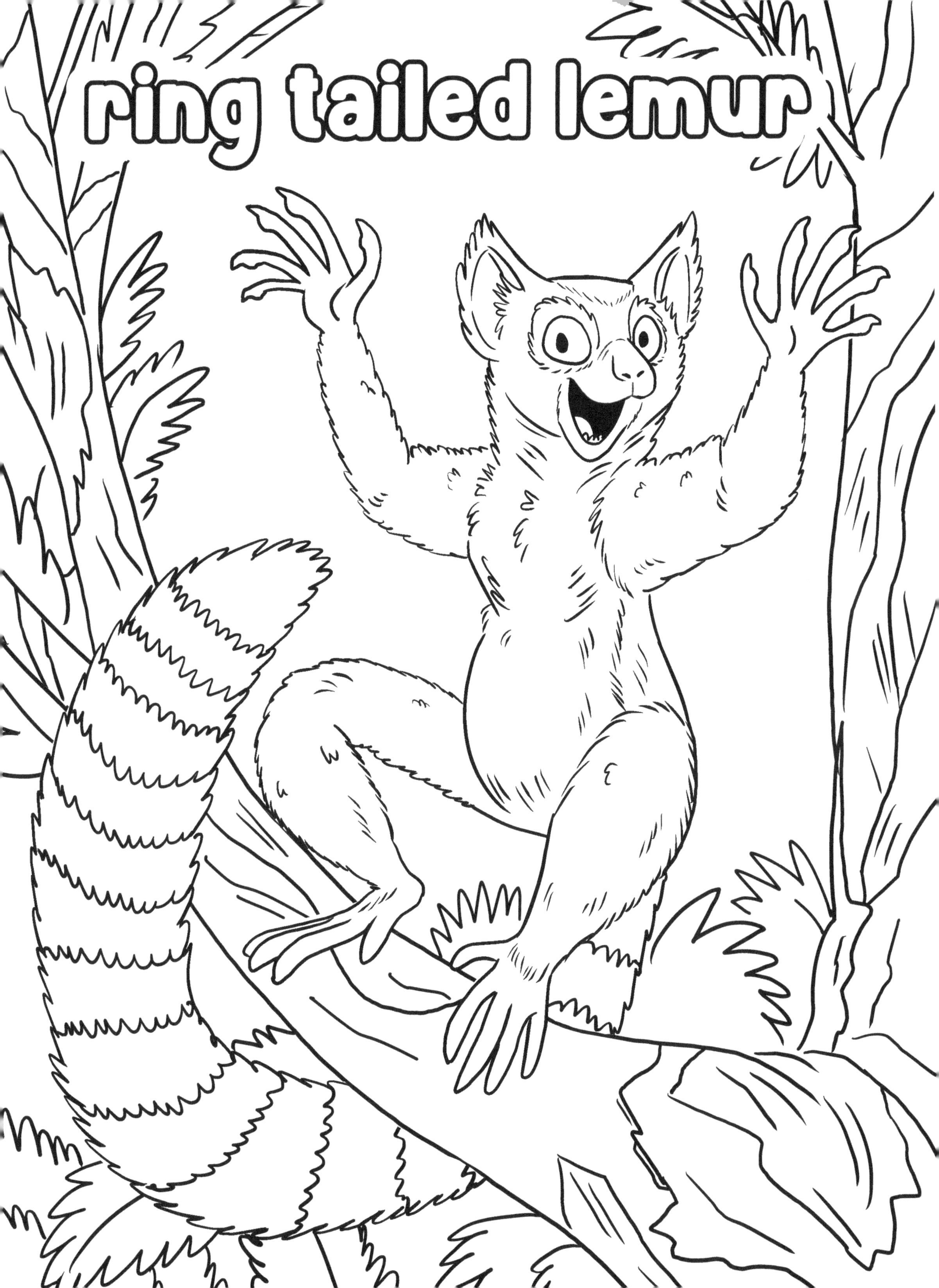
ring tailed lemur

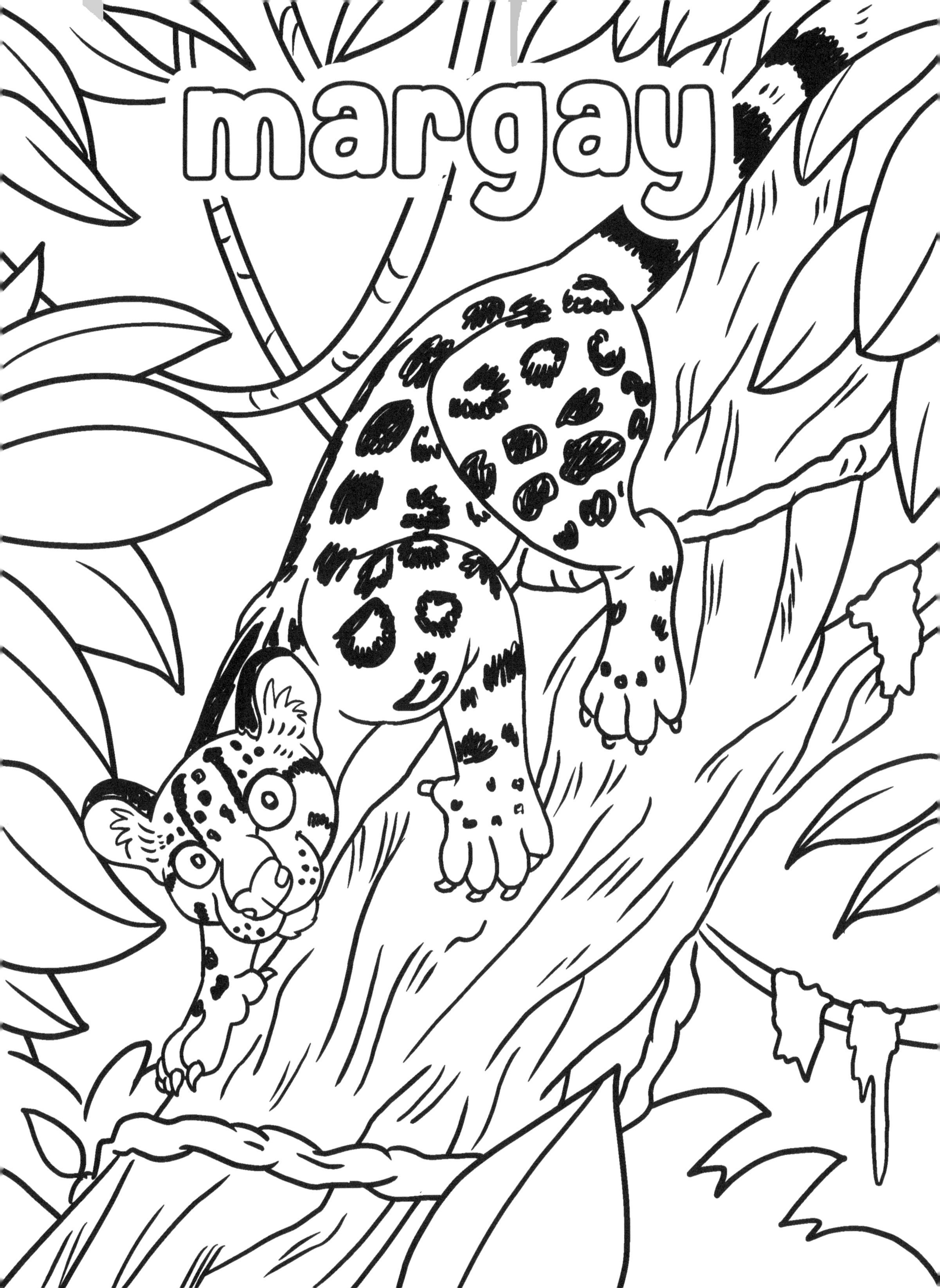
margay

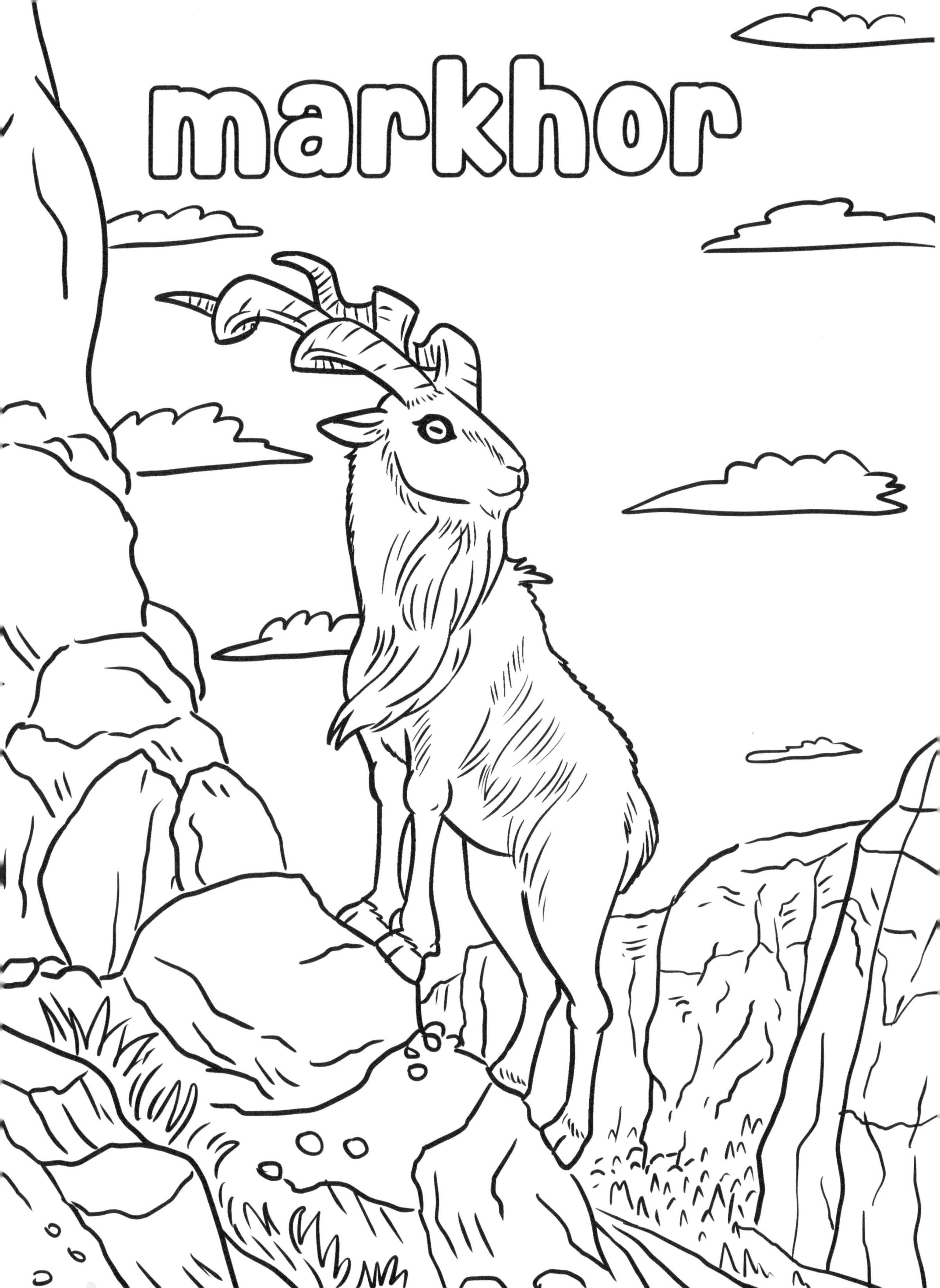
markhor

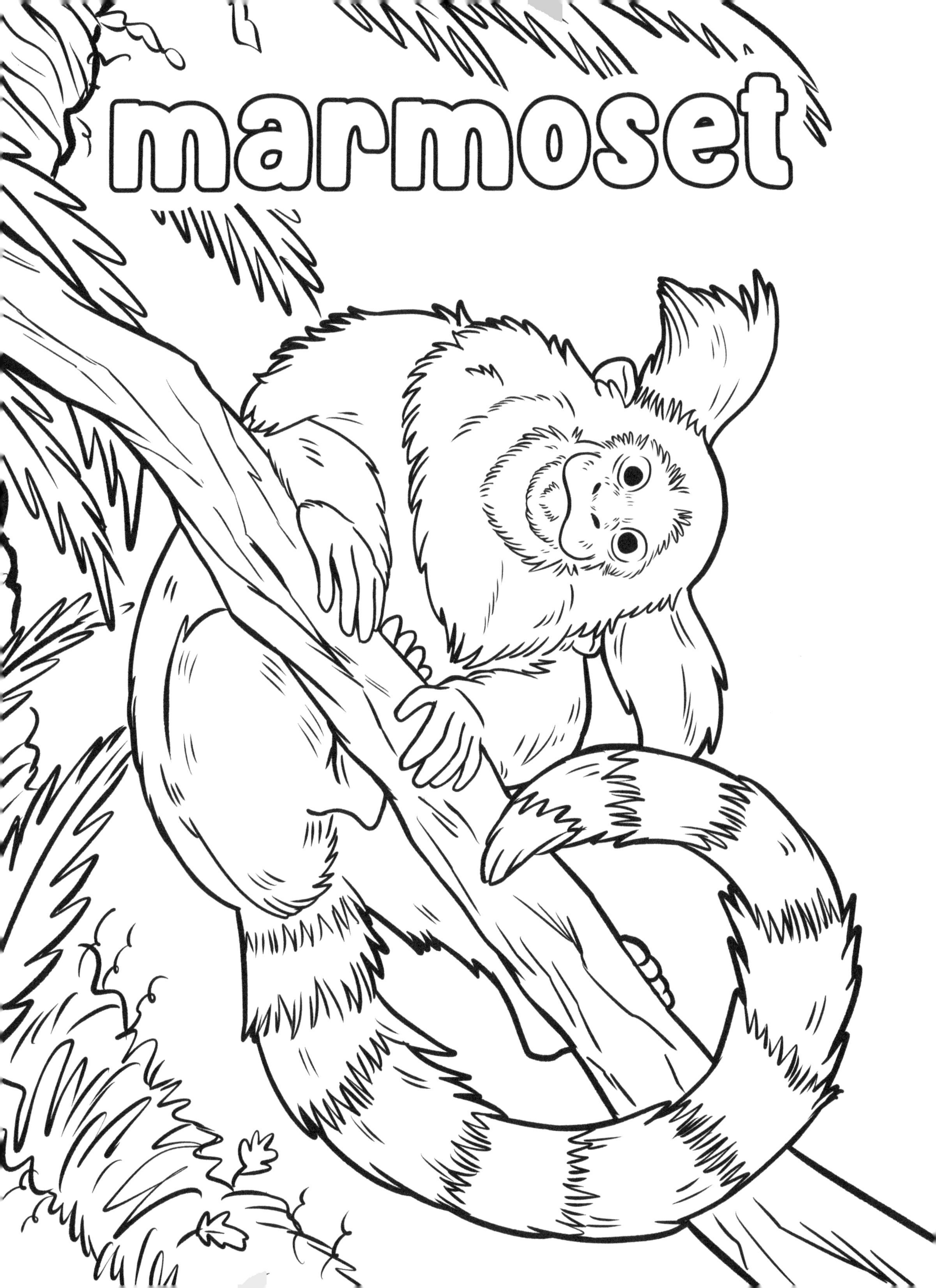
marmoset

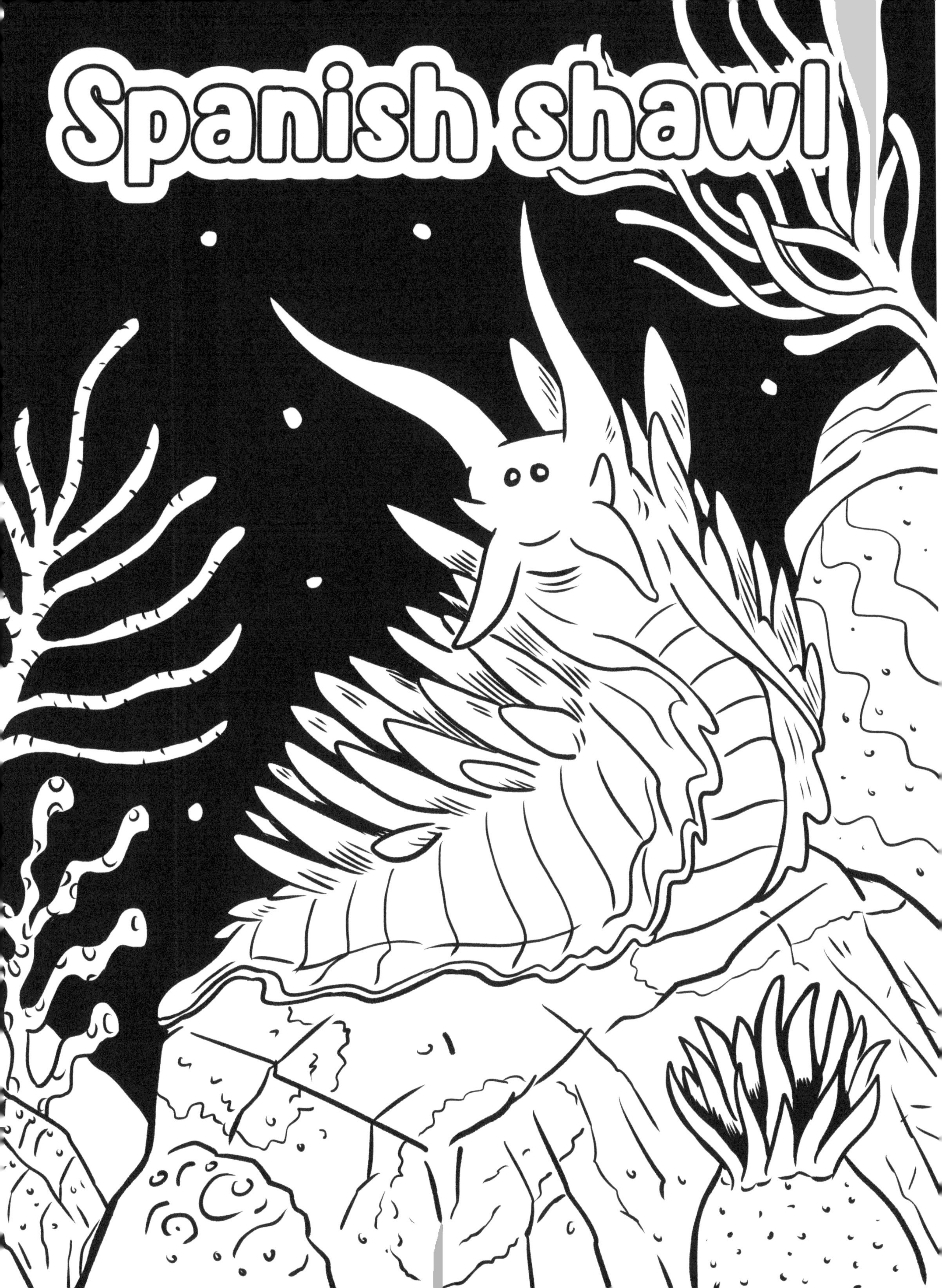
Spanish shawl

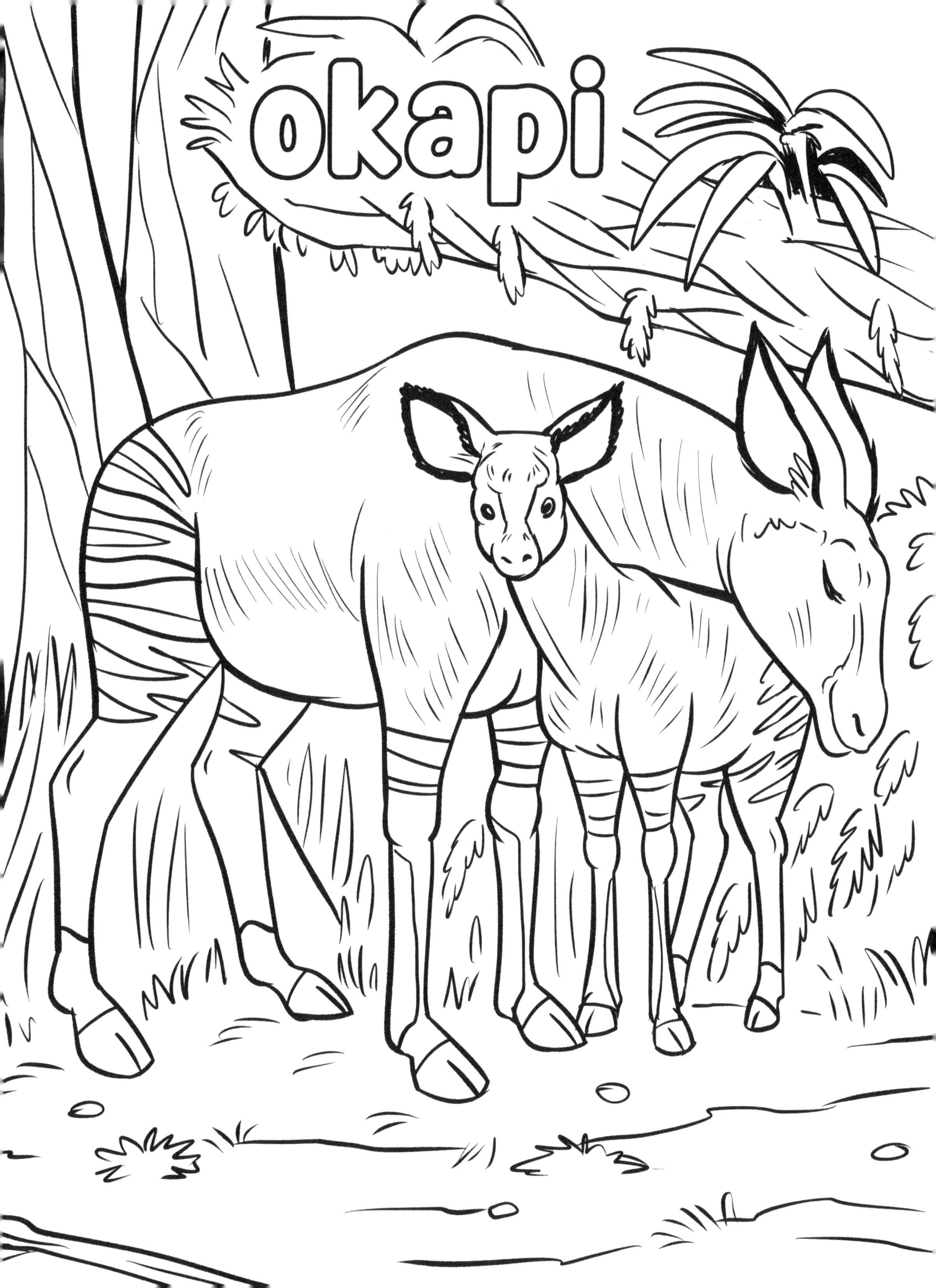
okapi

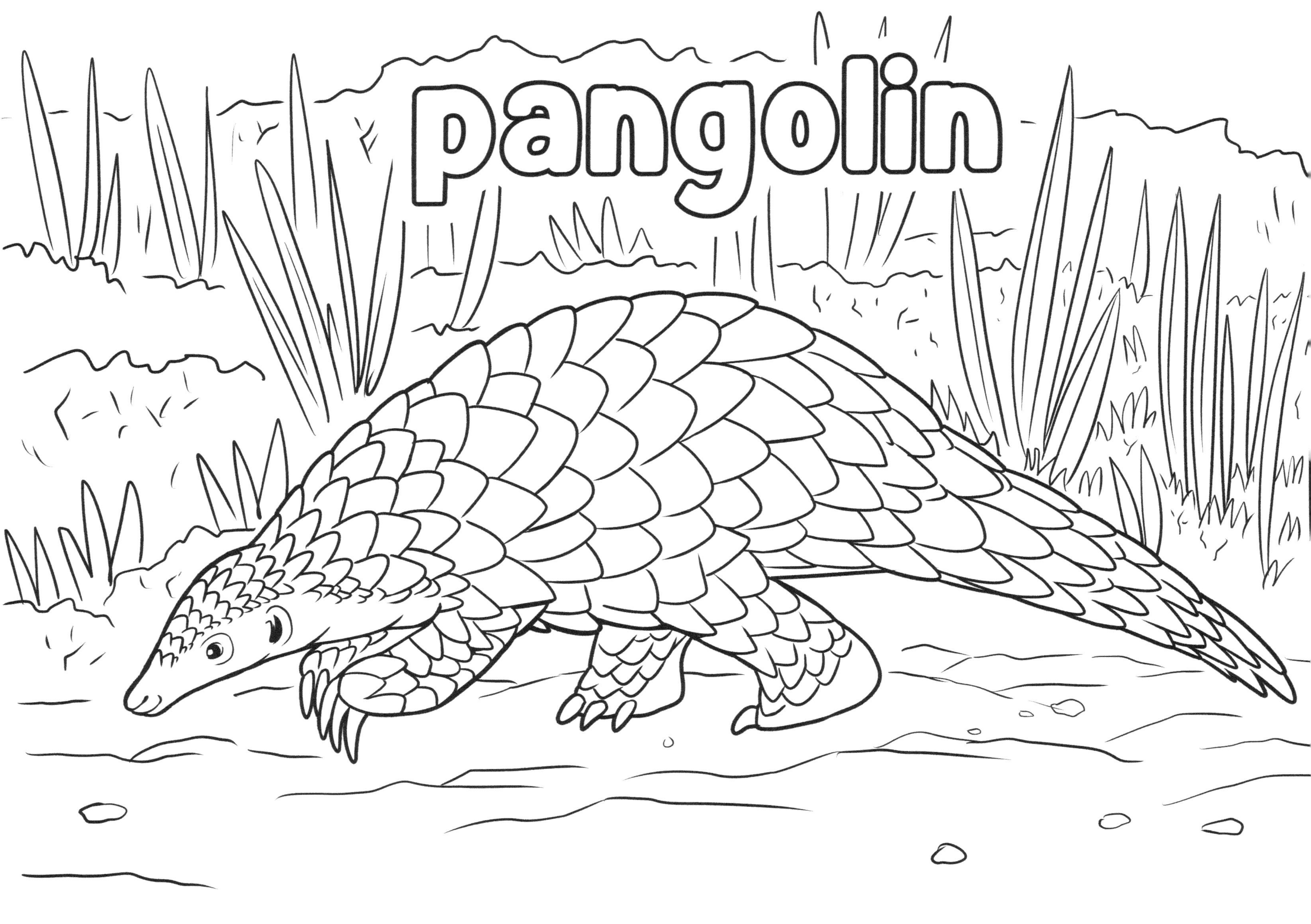
pangolin

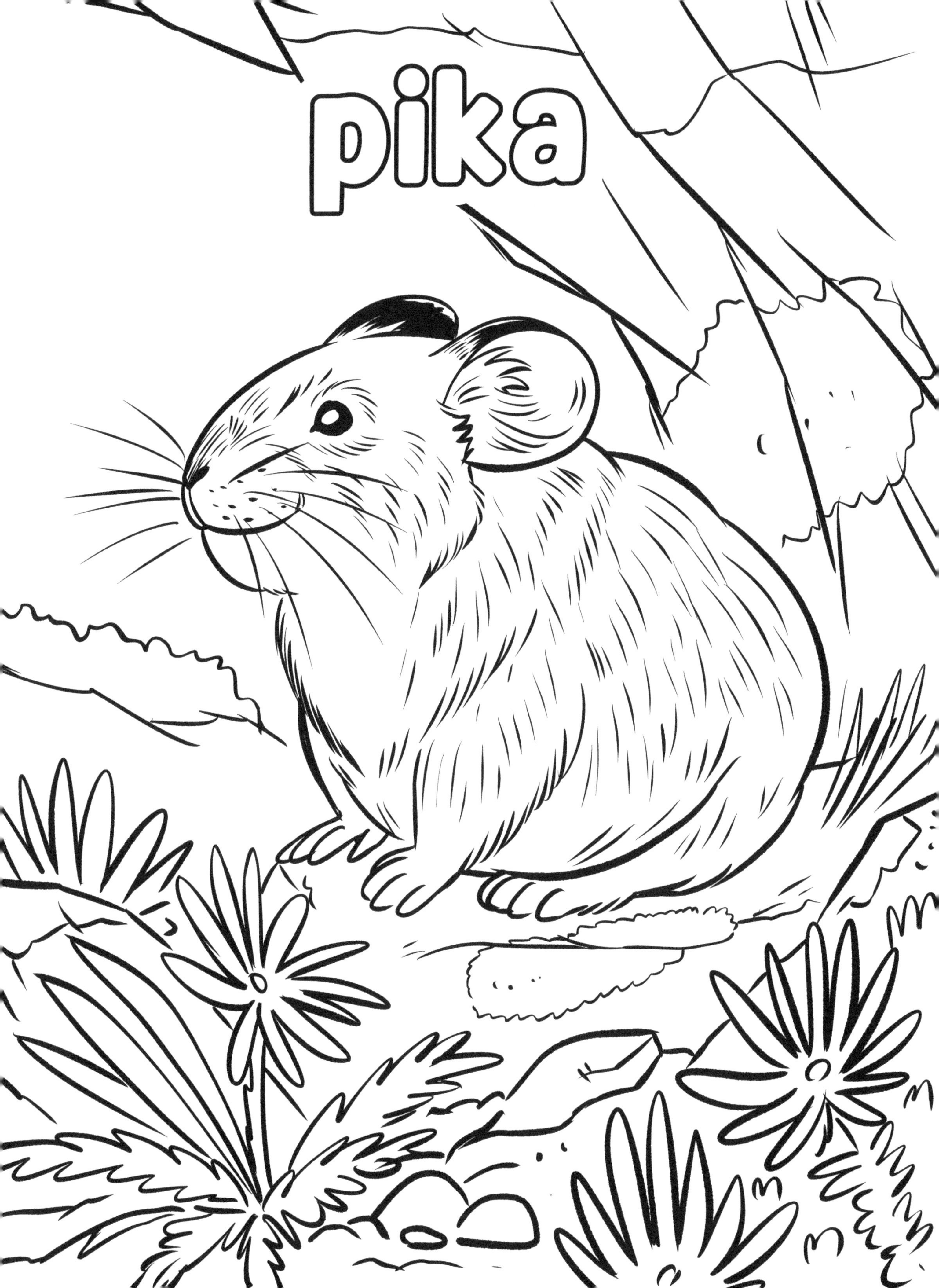
pika

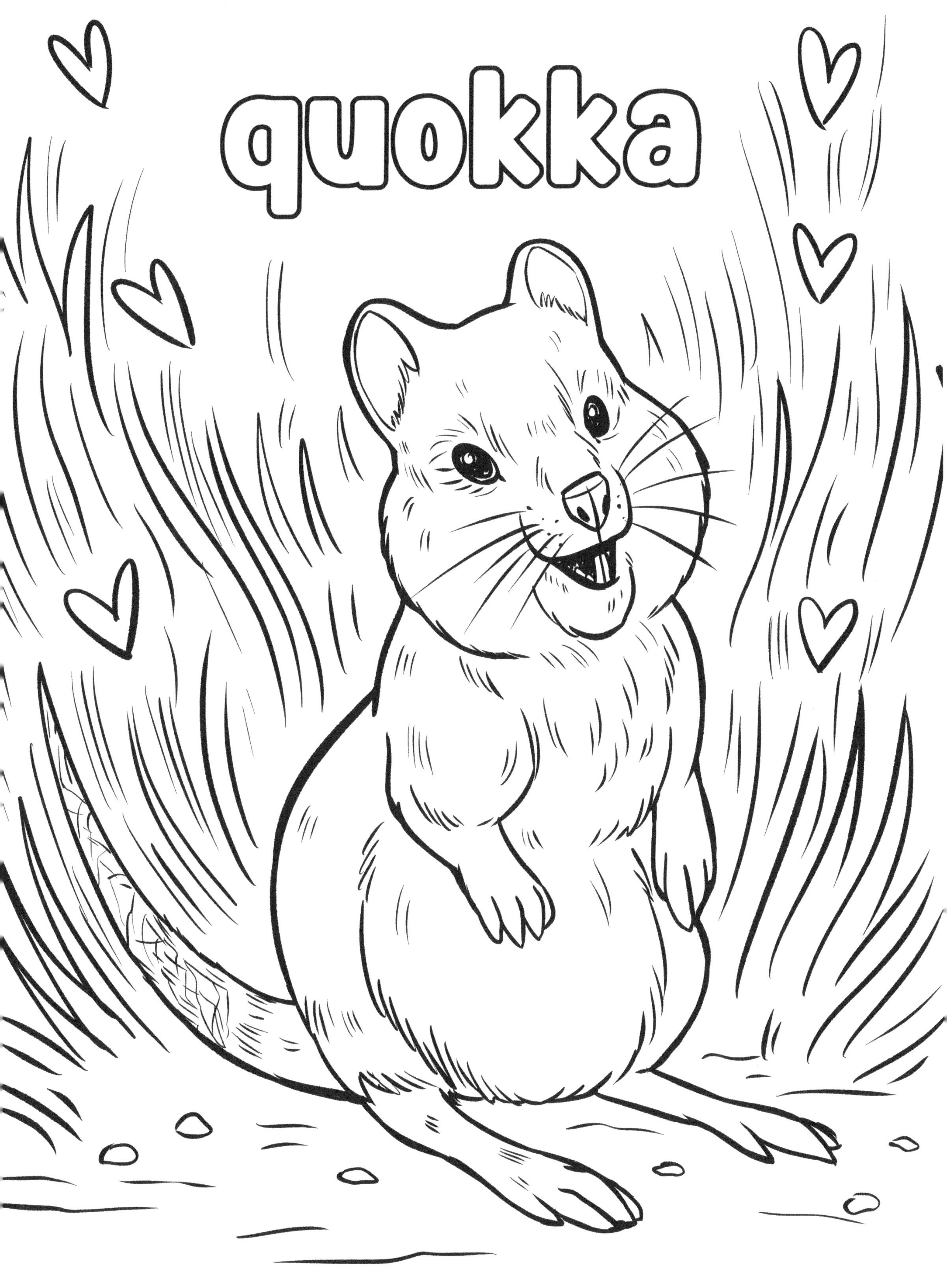
quokka

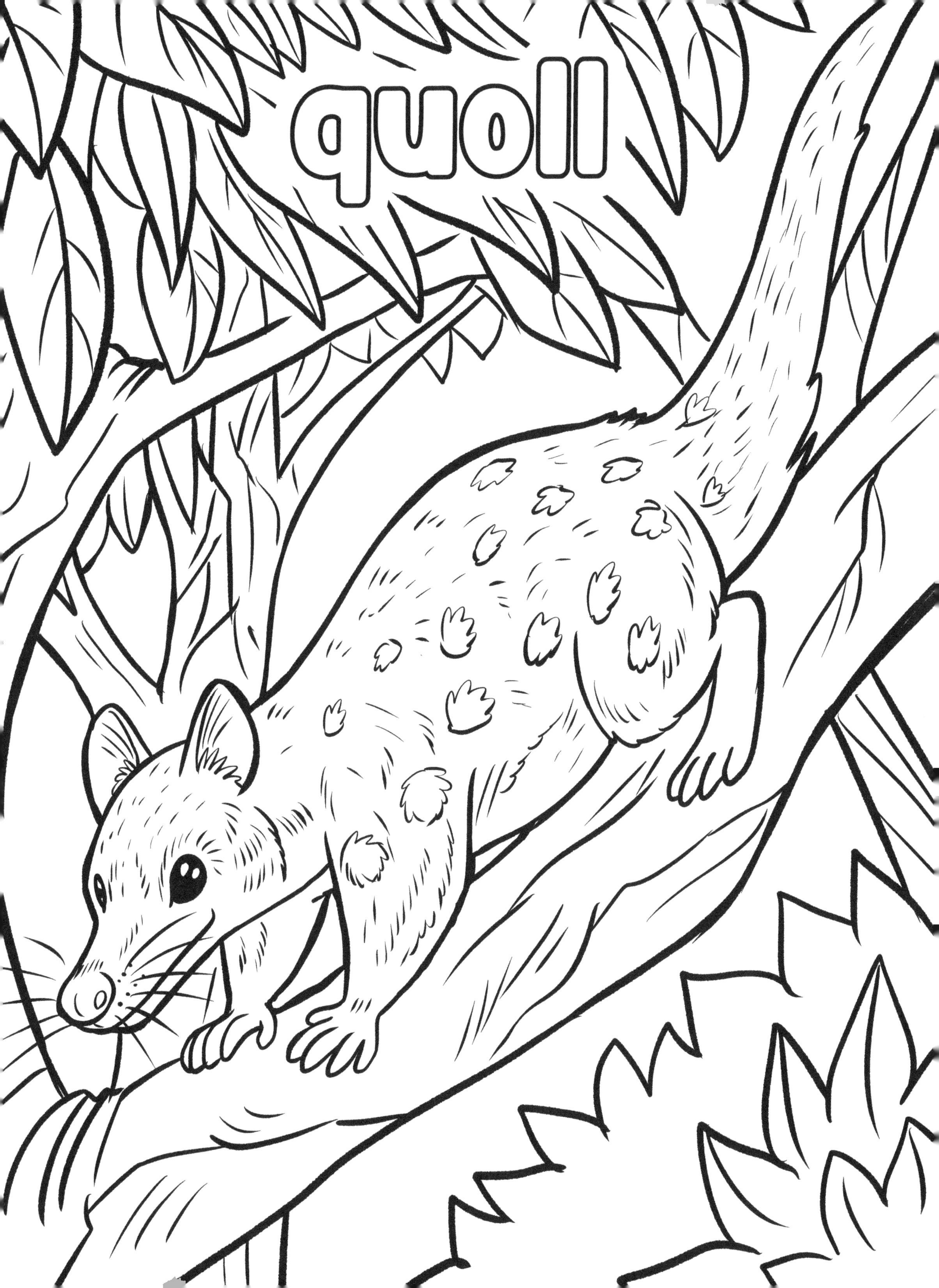
quoll

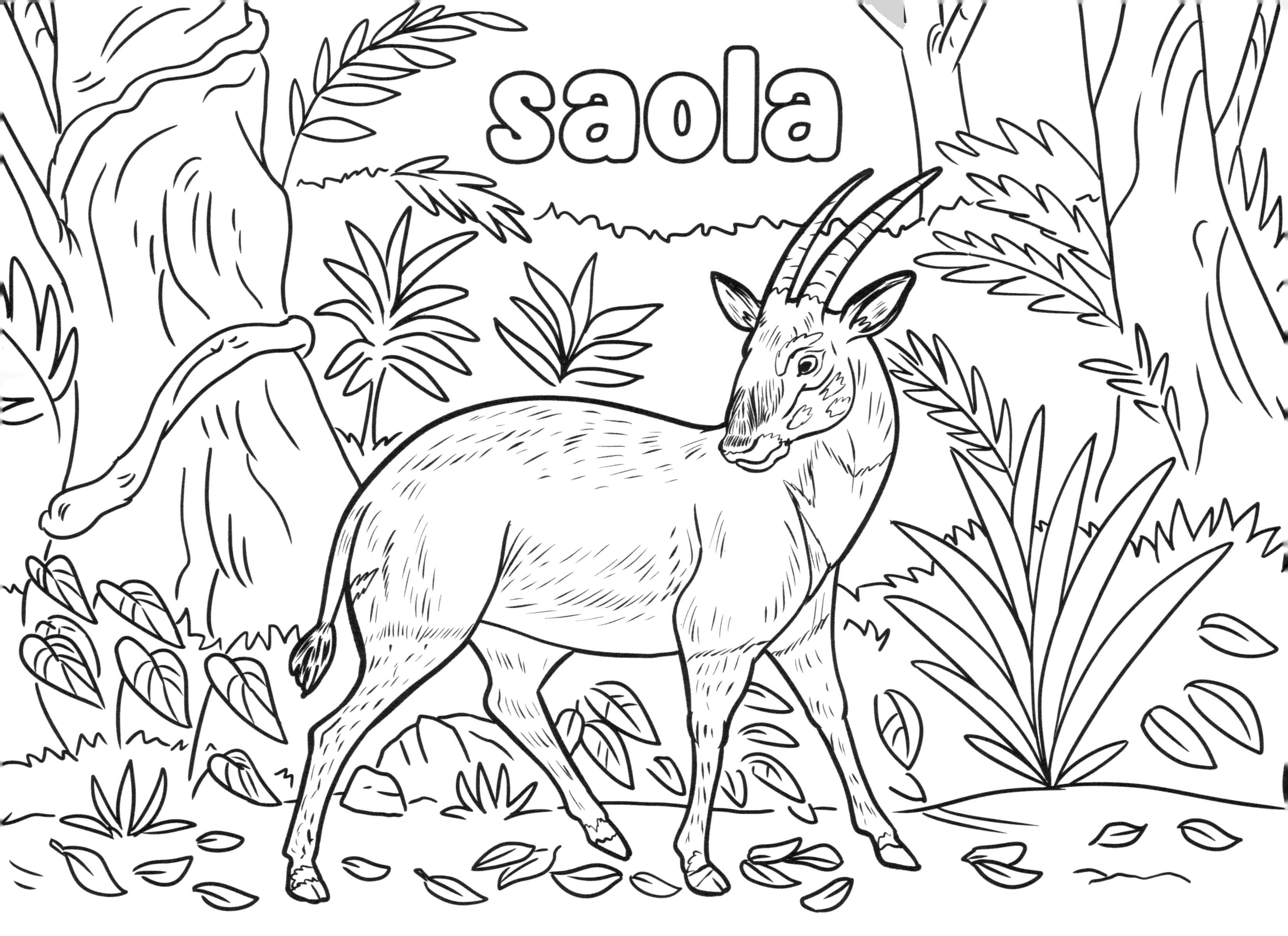
saola

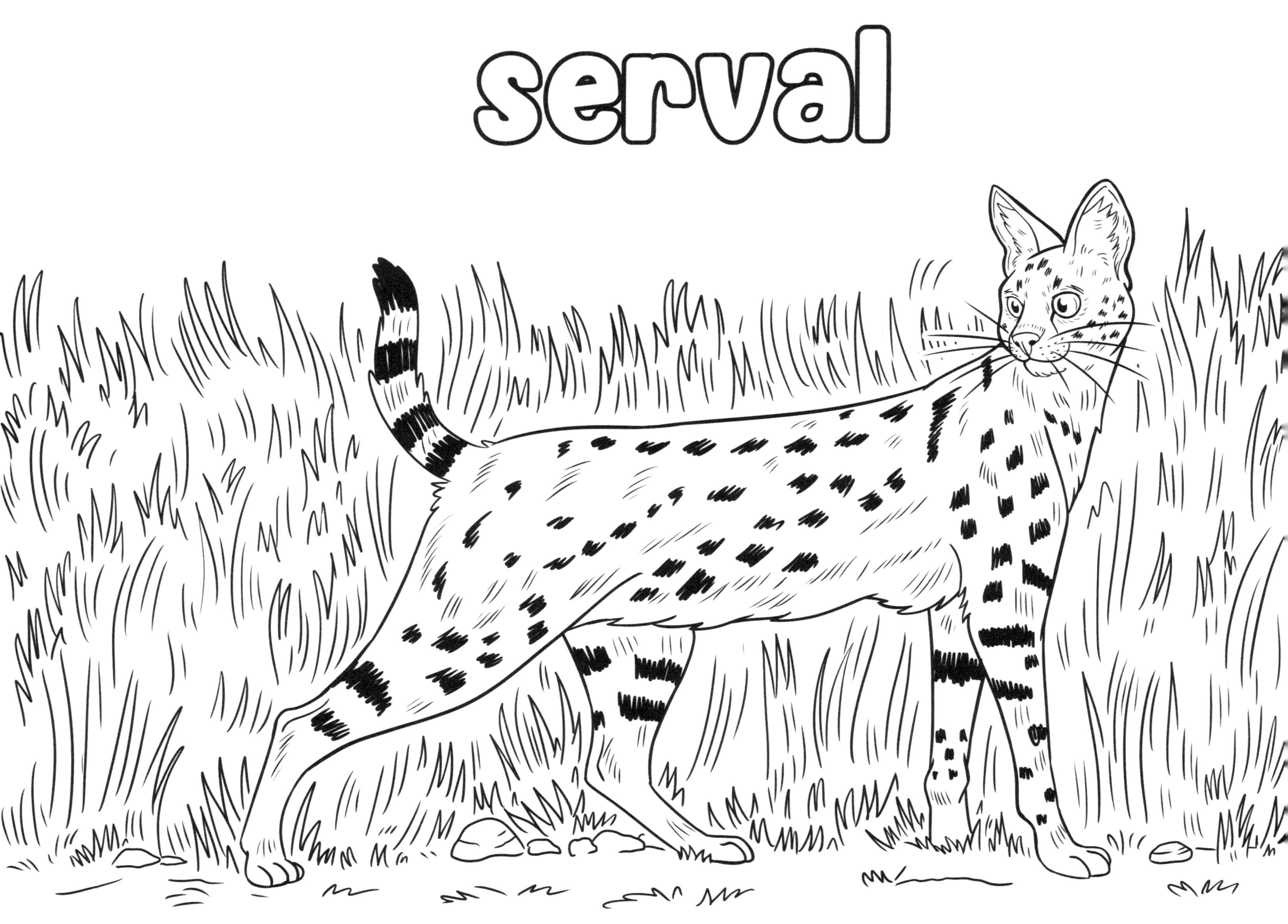
serval

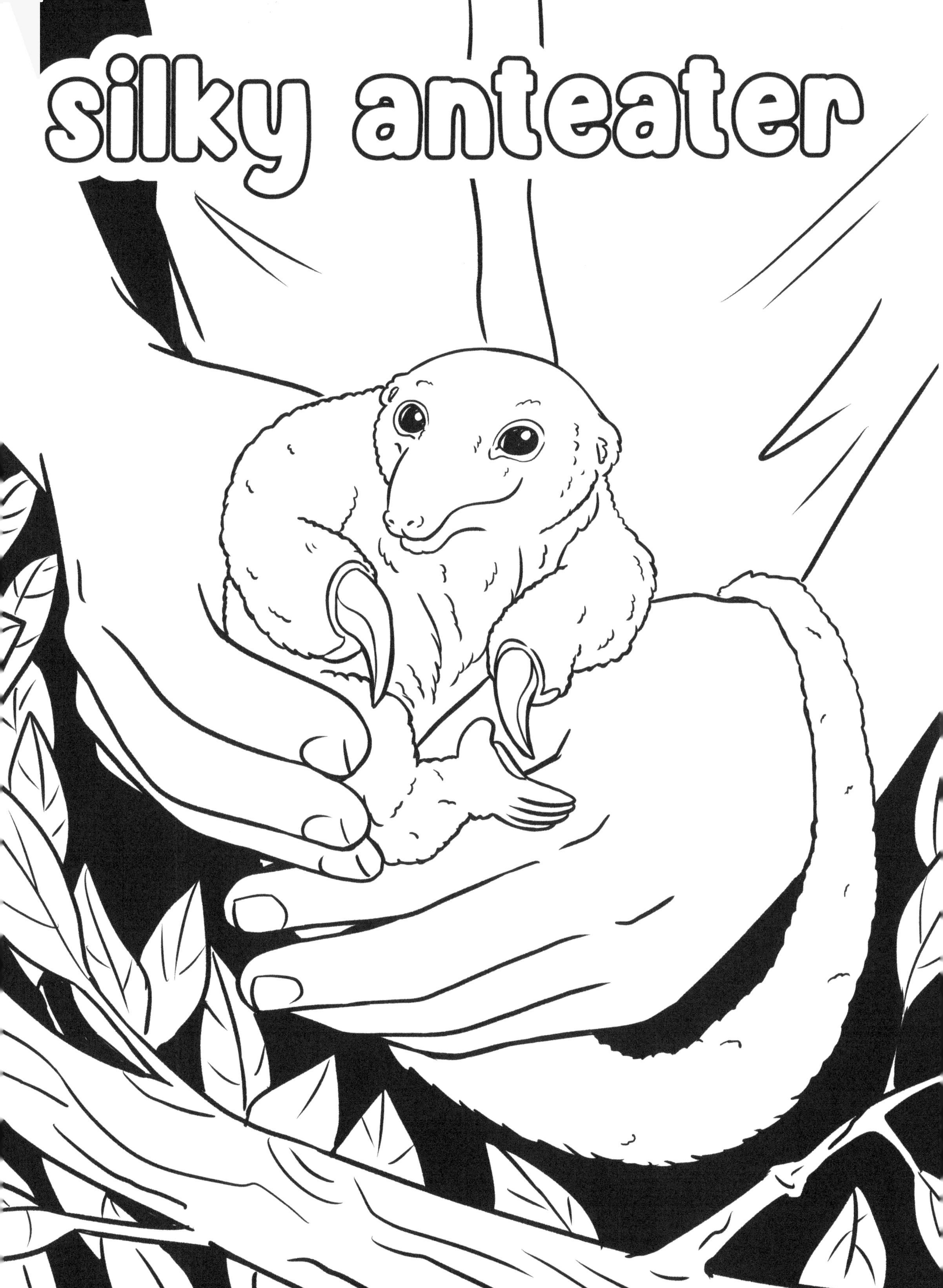
silky anteater

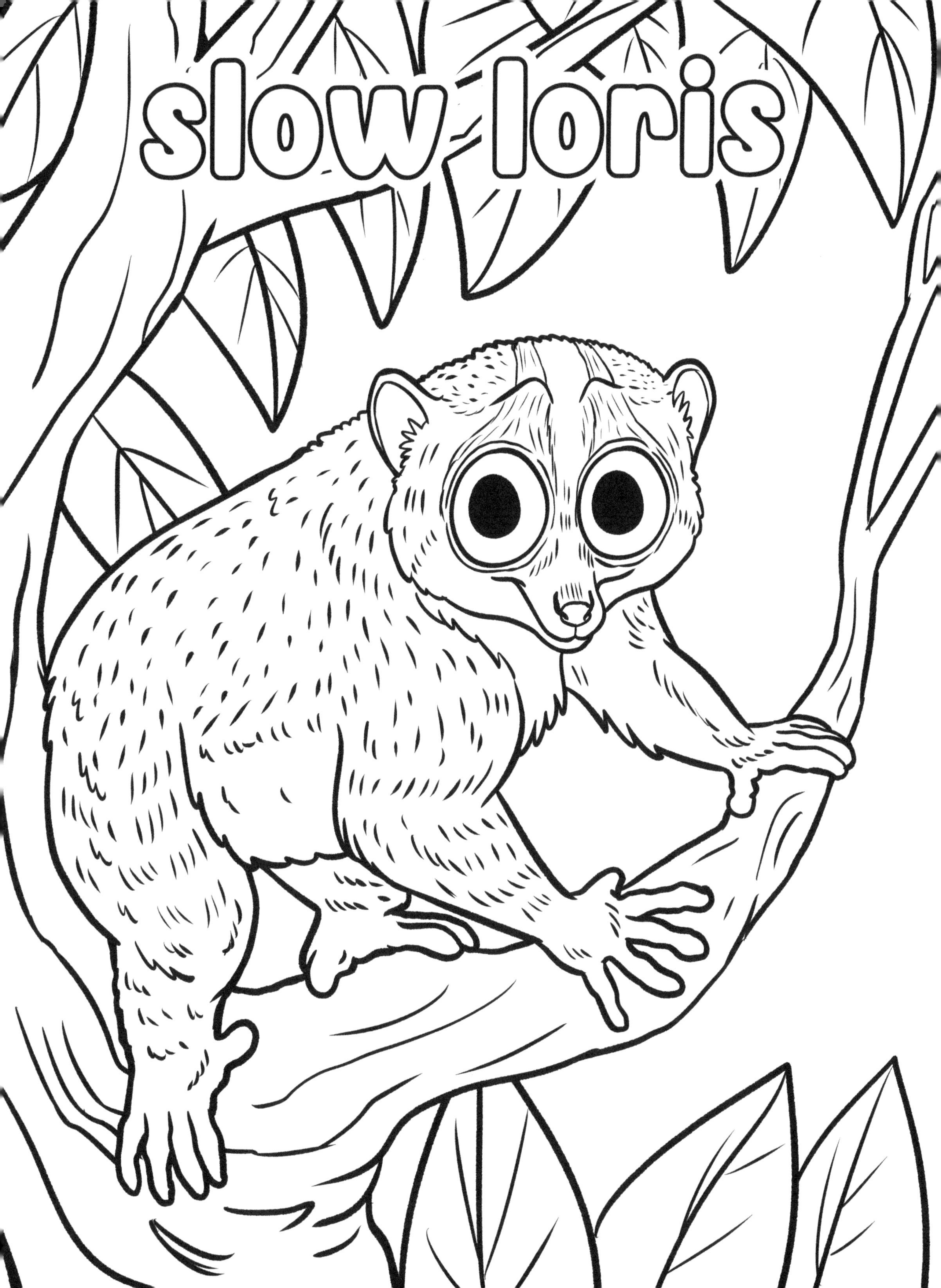
slow loris

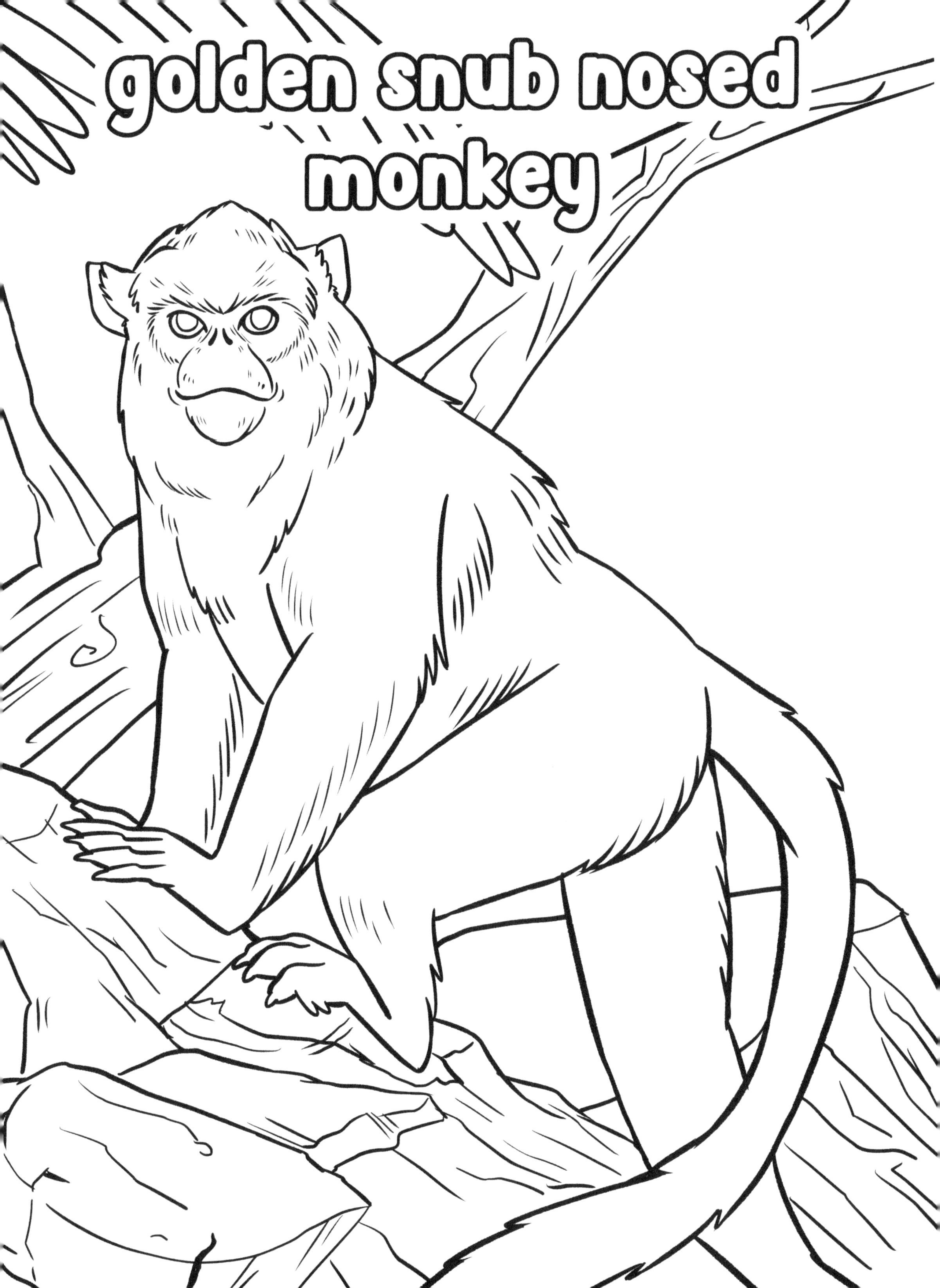
golden snub nosed
monkey

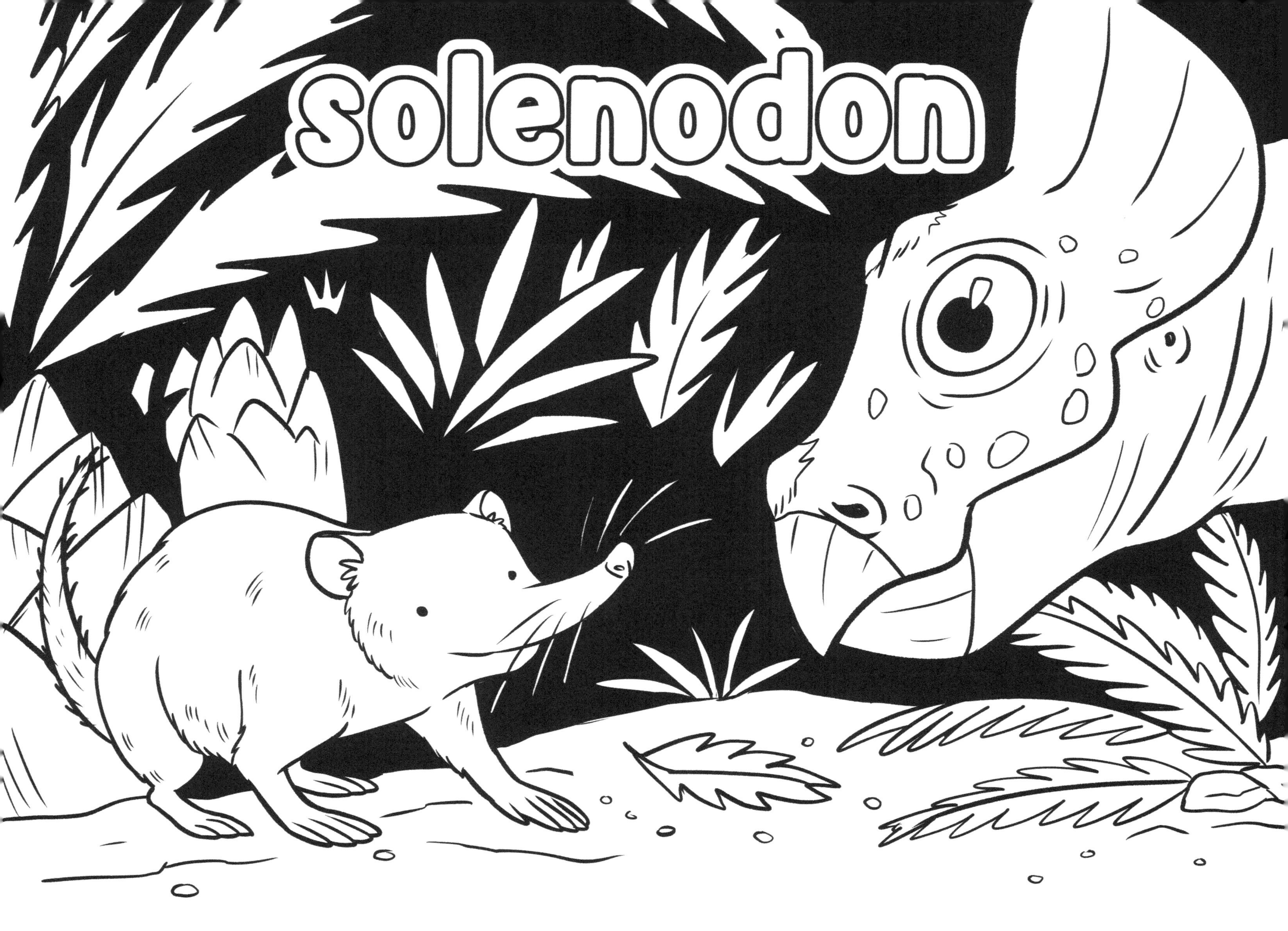
solenodon

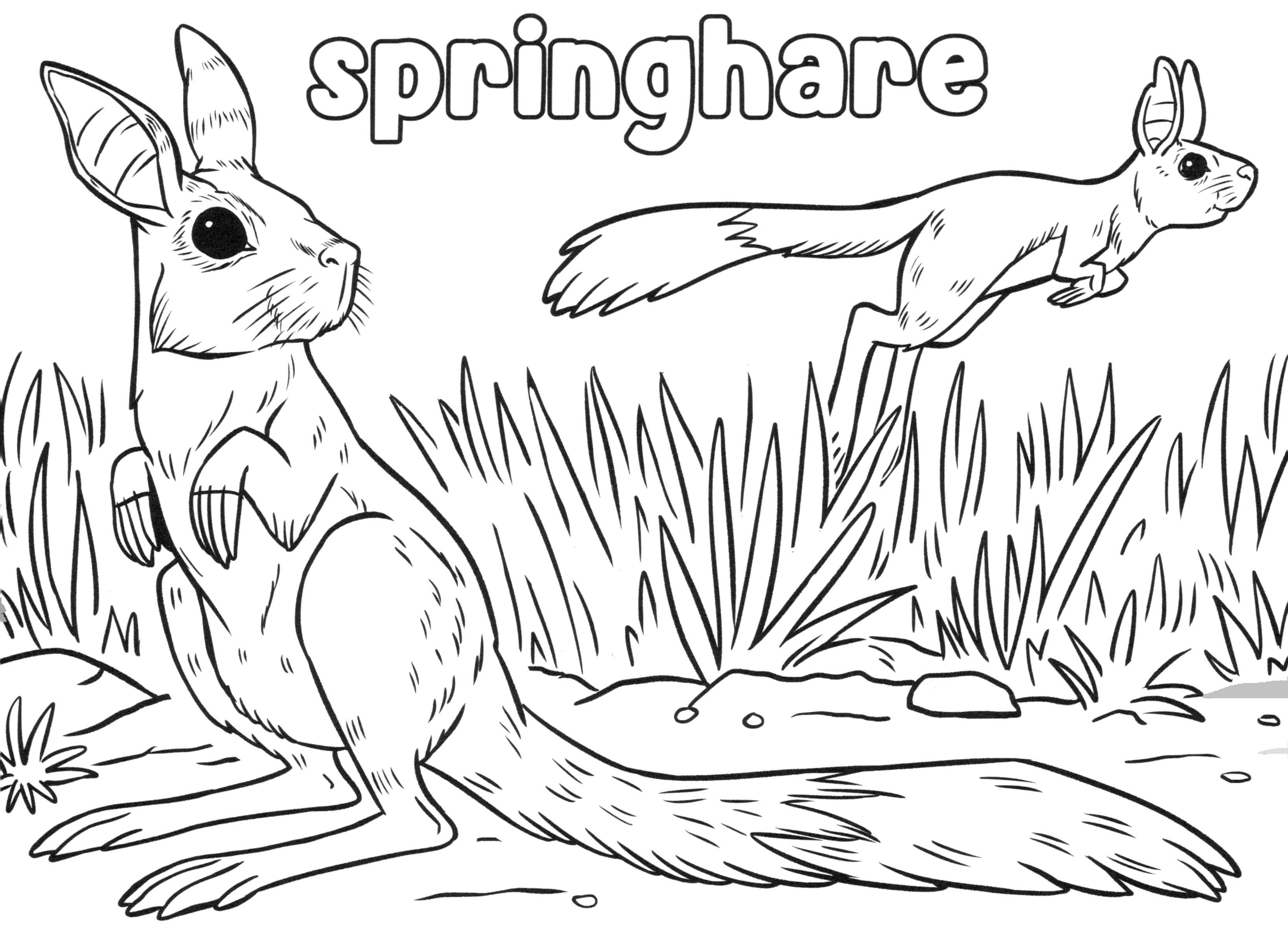
springhare

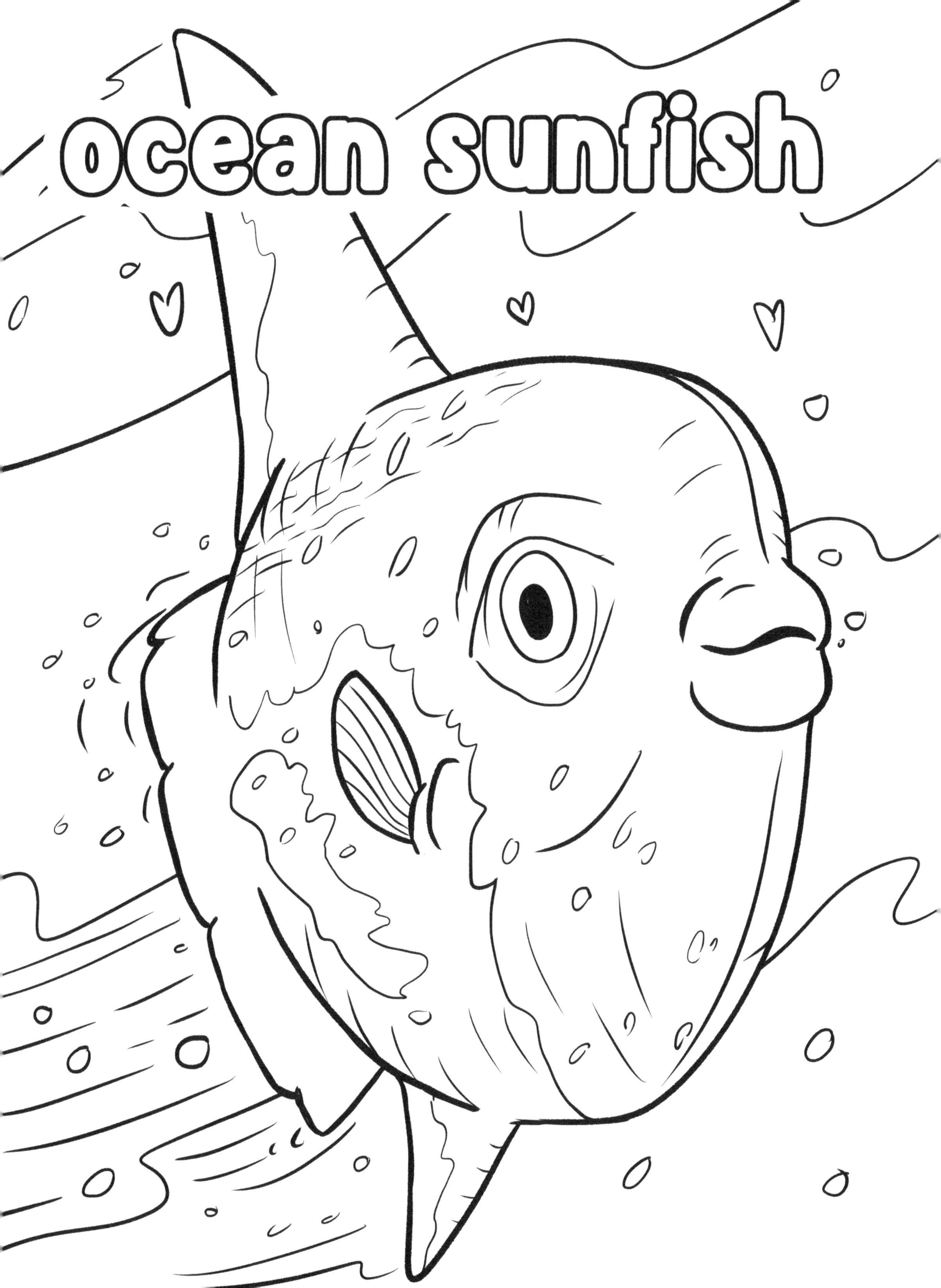
ocean sunfish

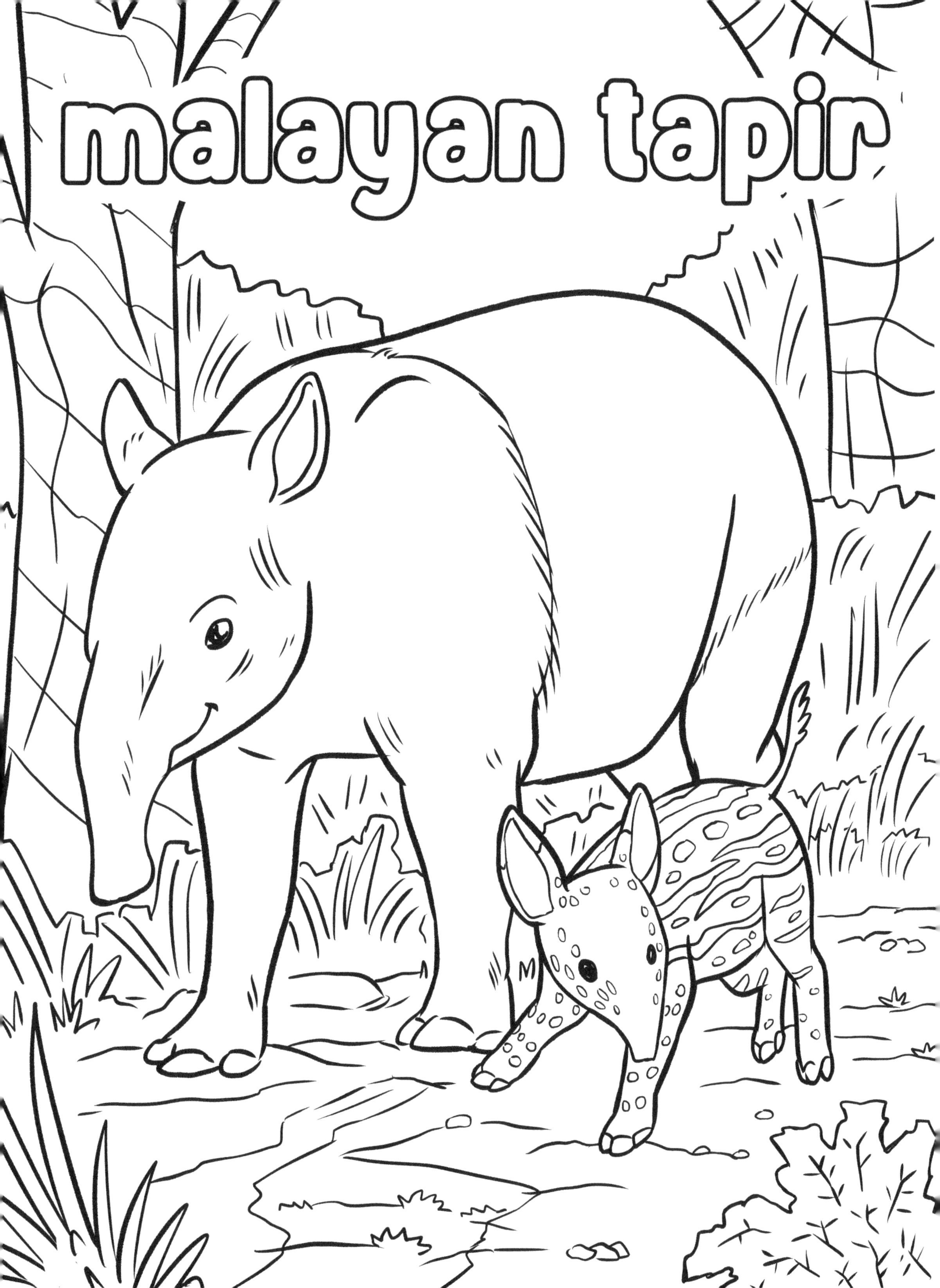
malayan tapir

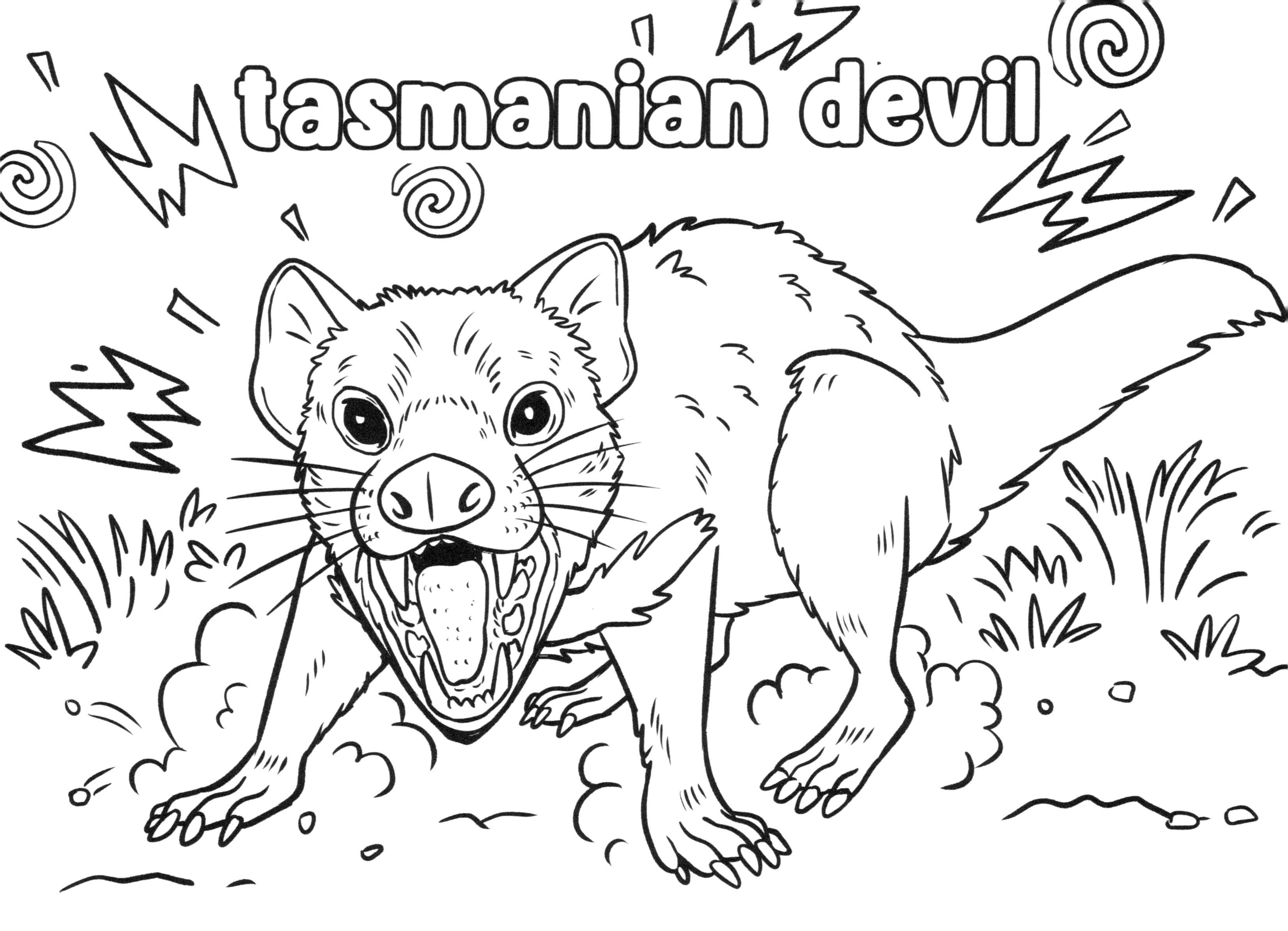
tasmanian devil

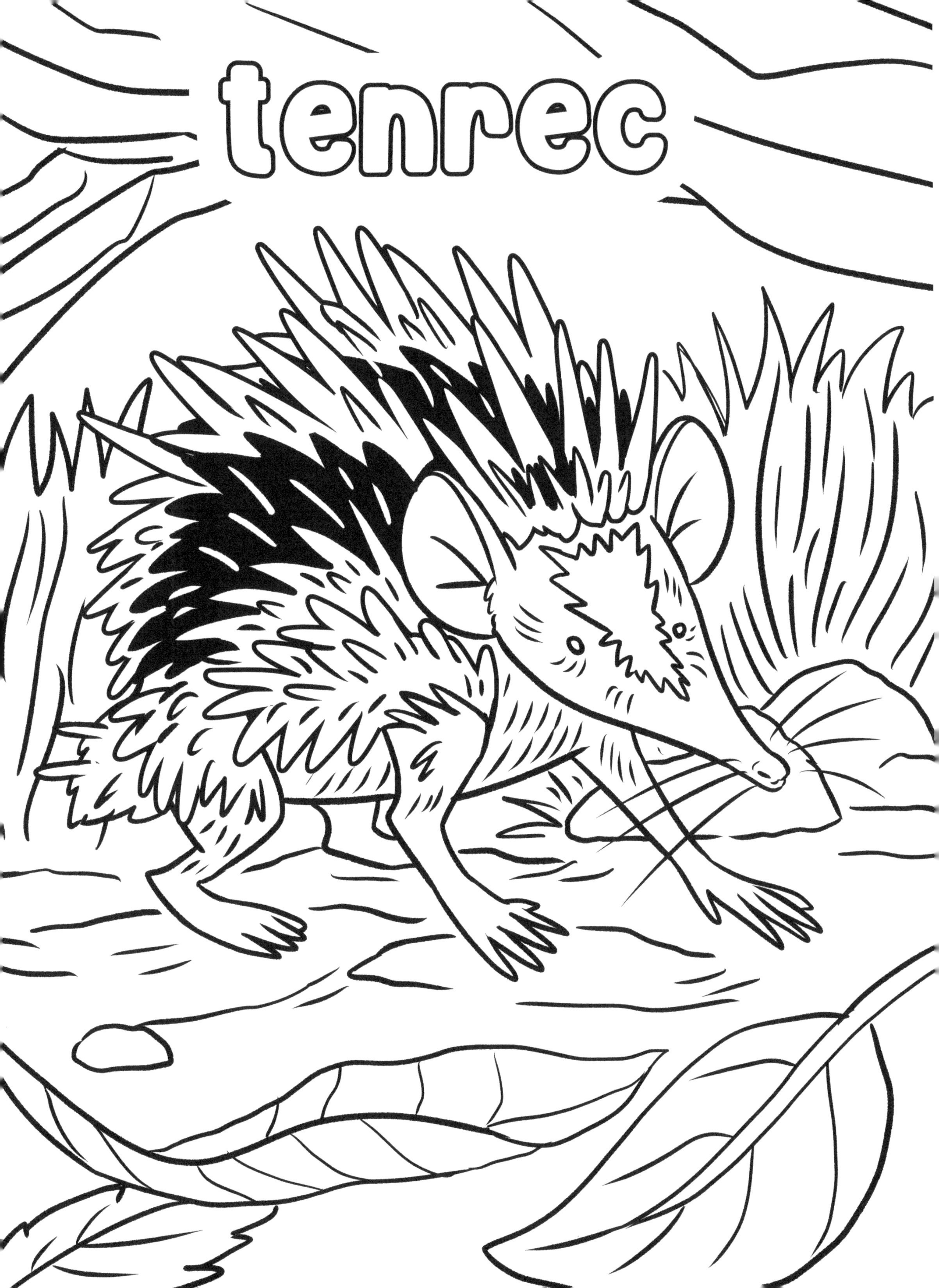
tenrec

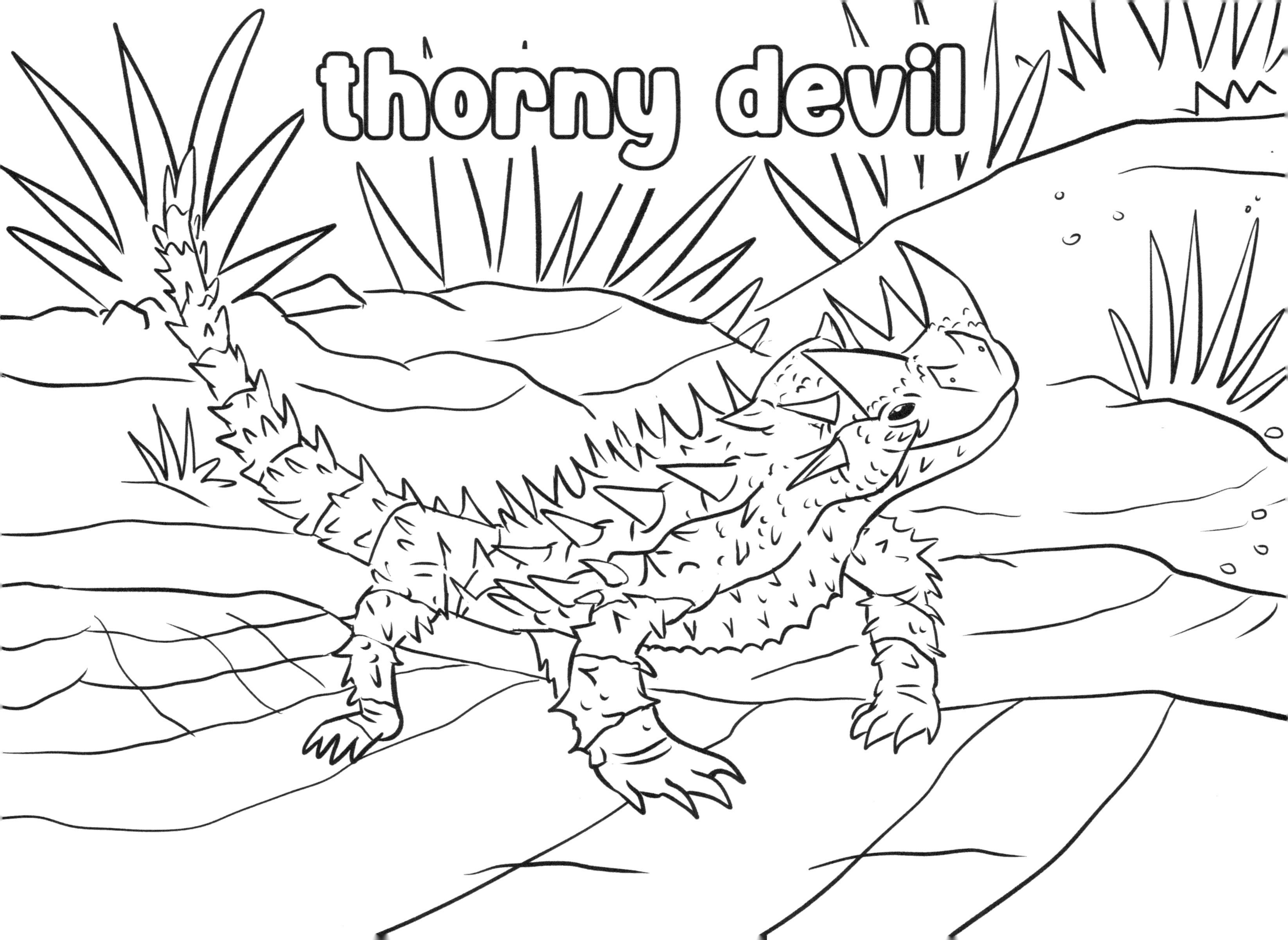
thorny devil

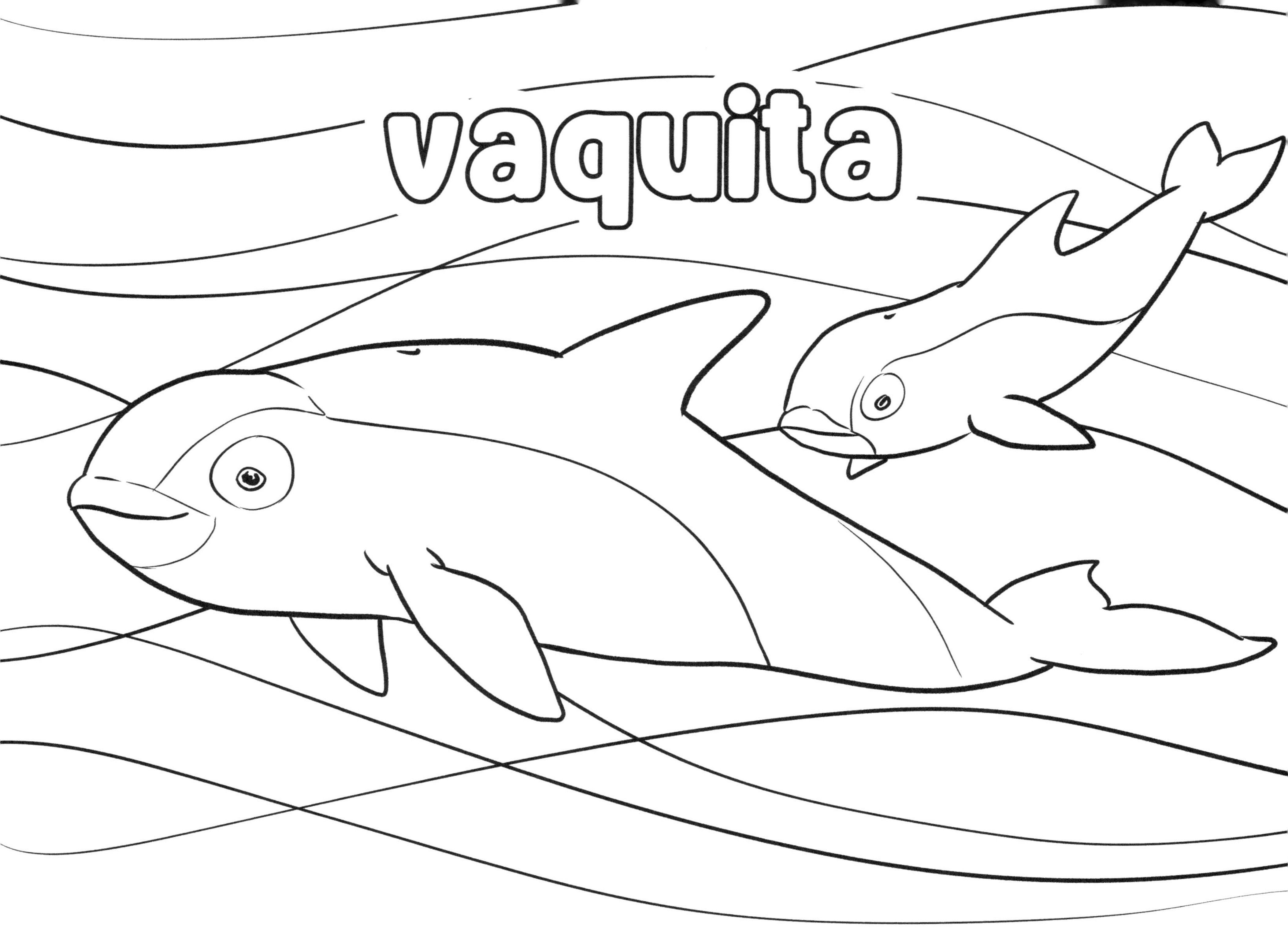
vaquita

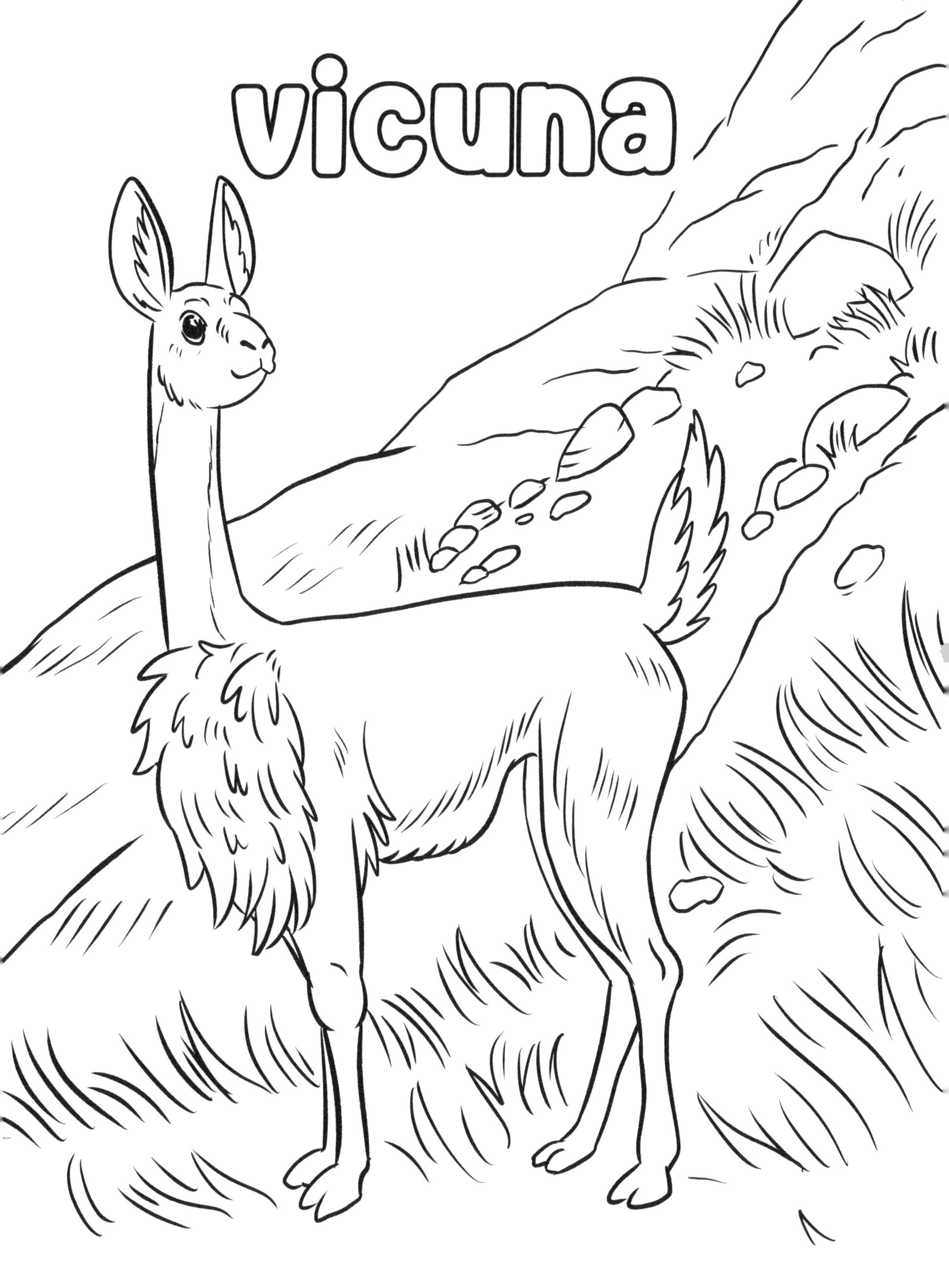
vicuna

southern viscacha

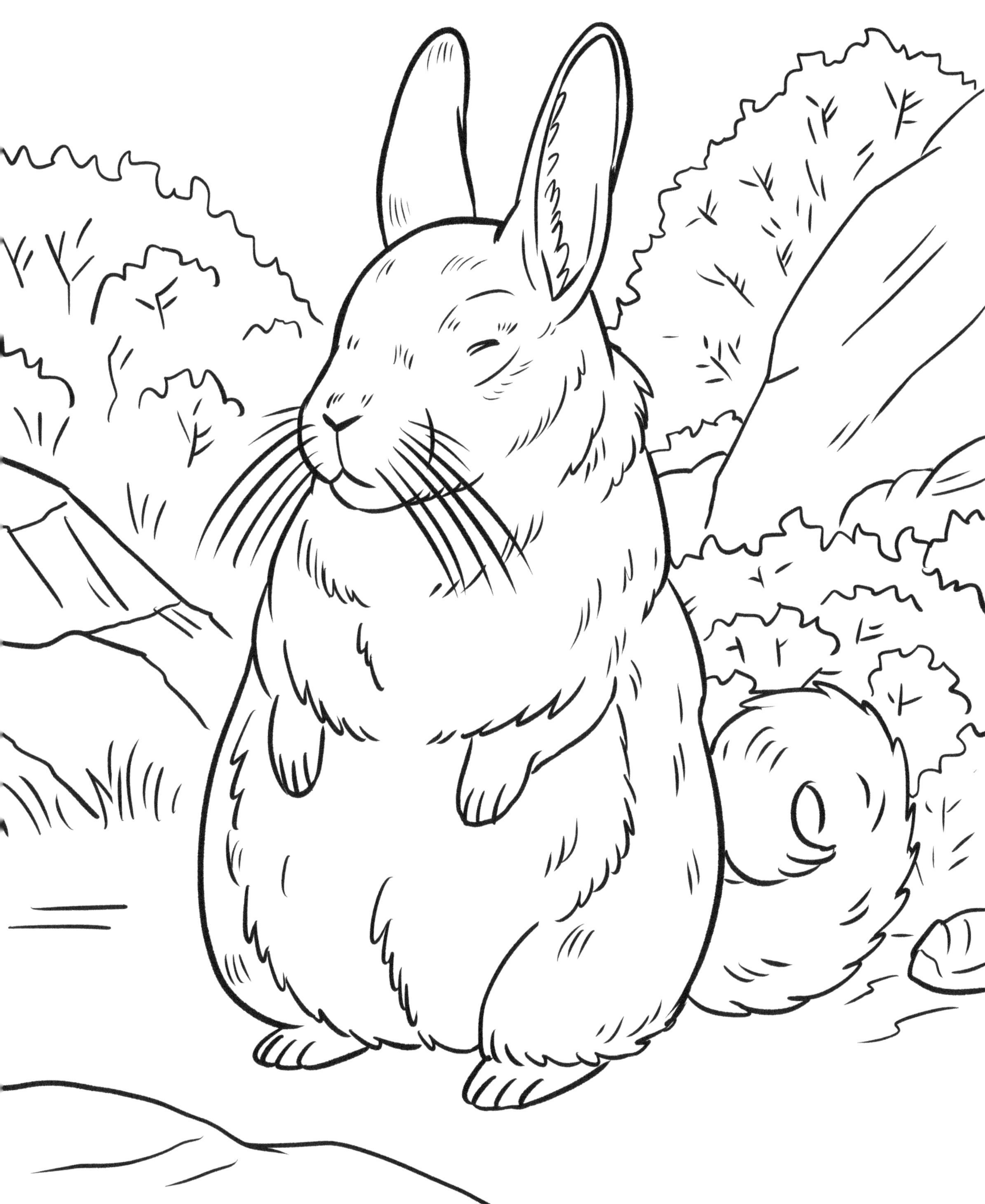

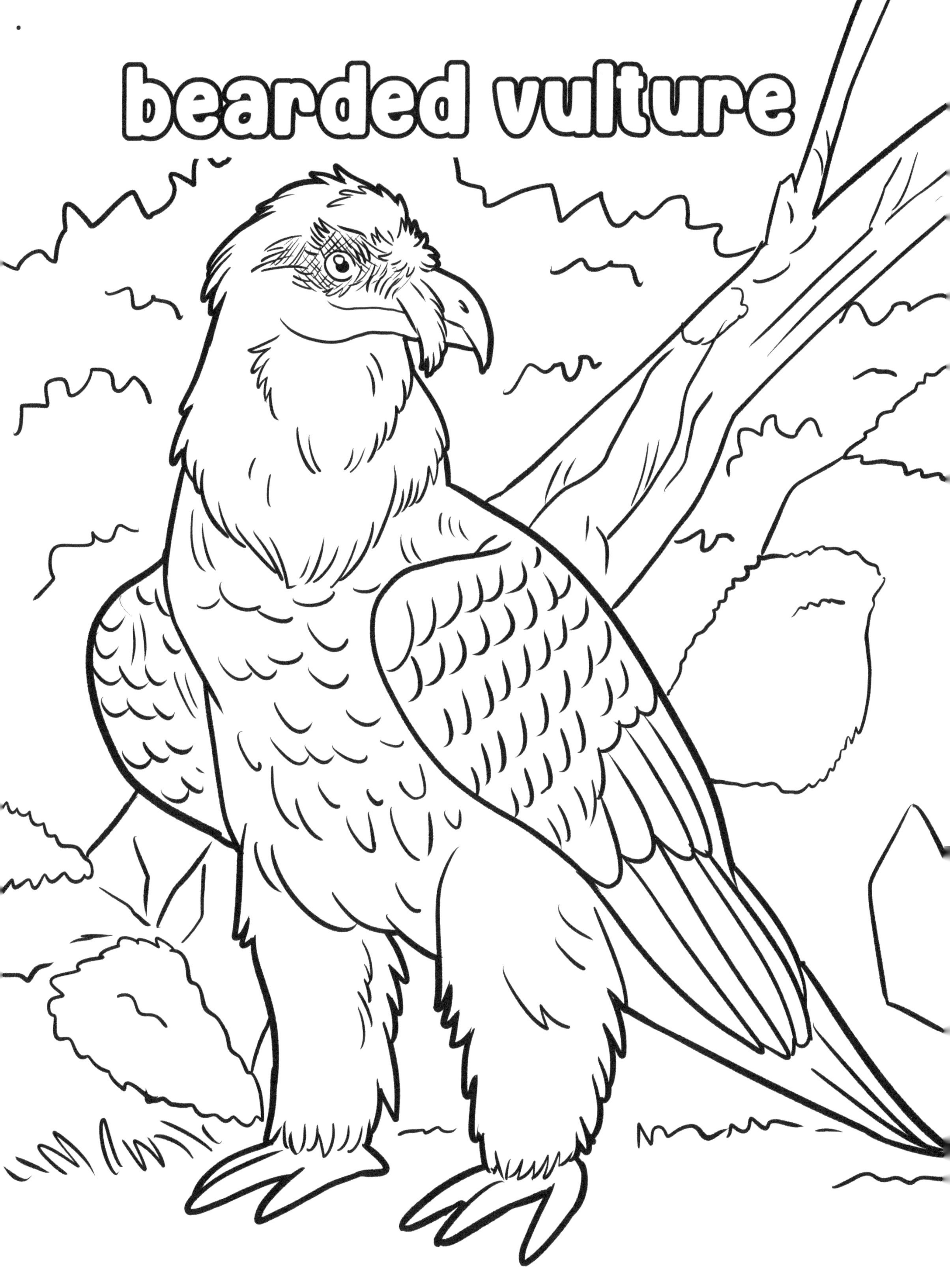
bearded vulture

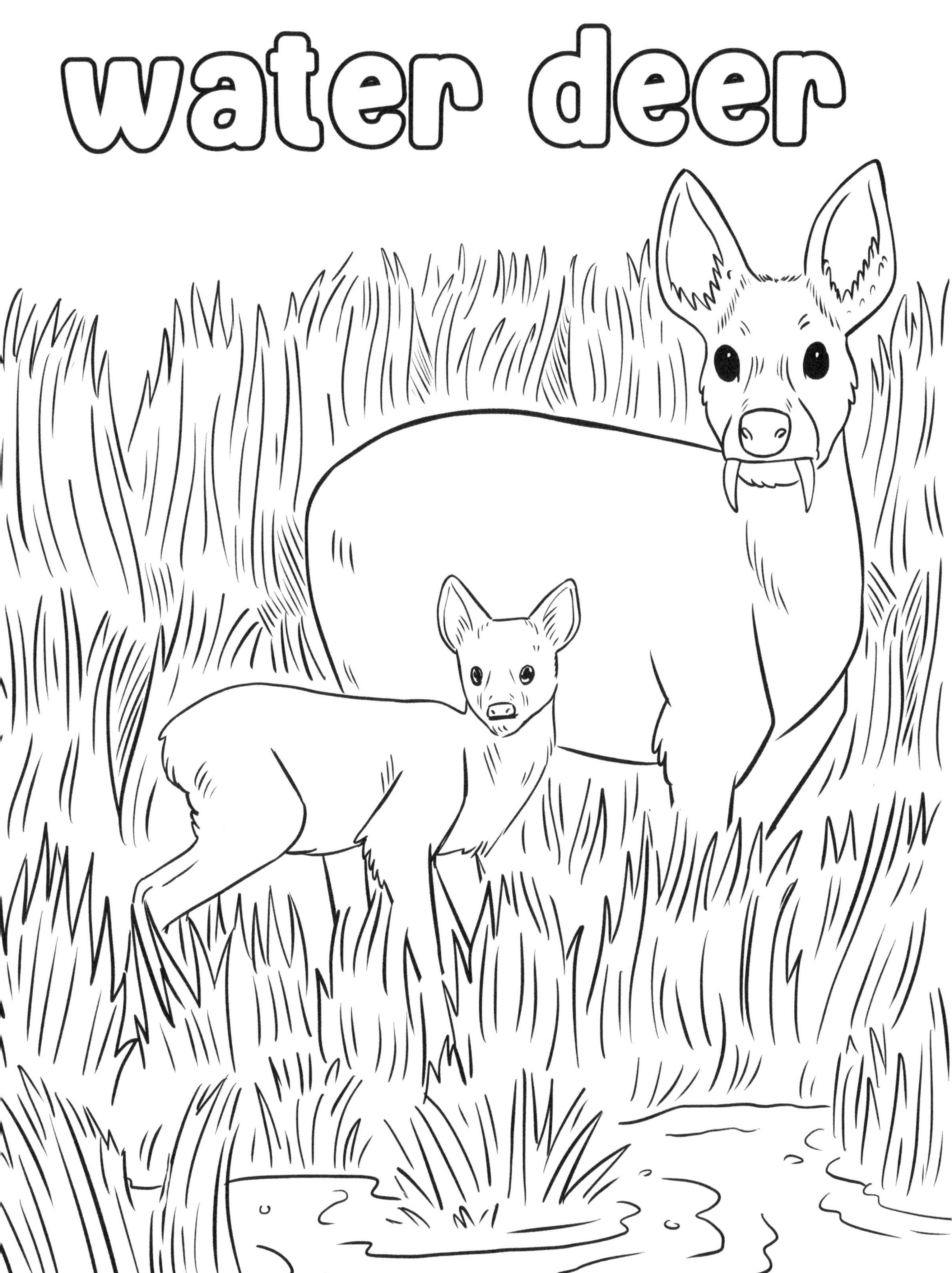
water deer

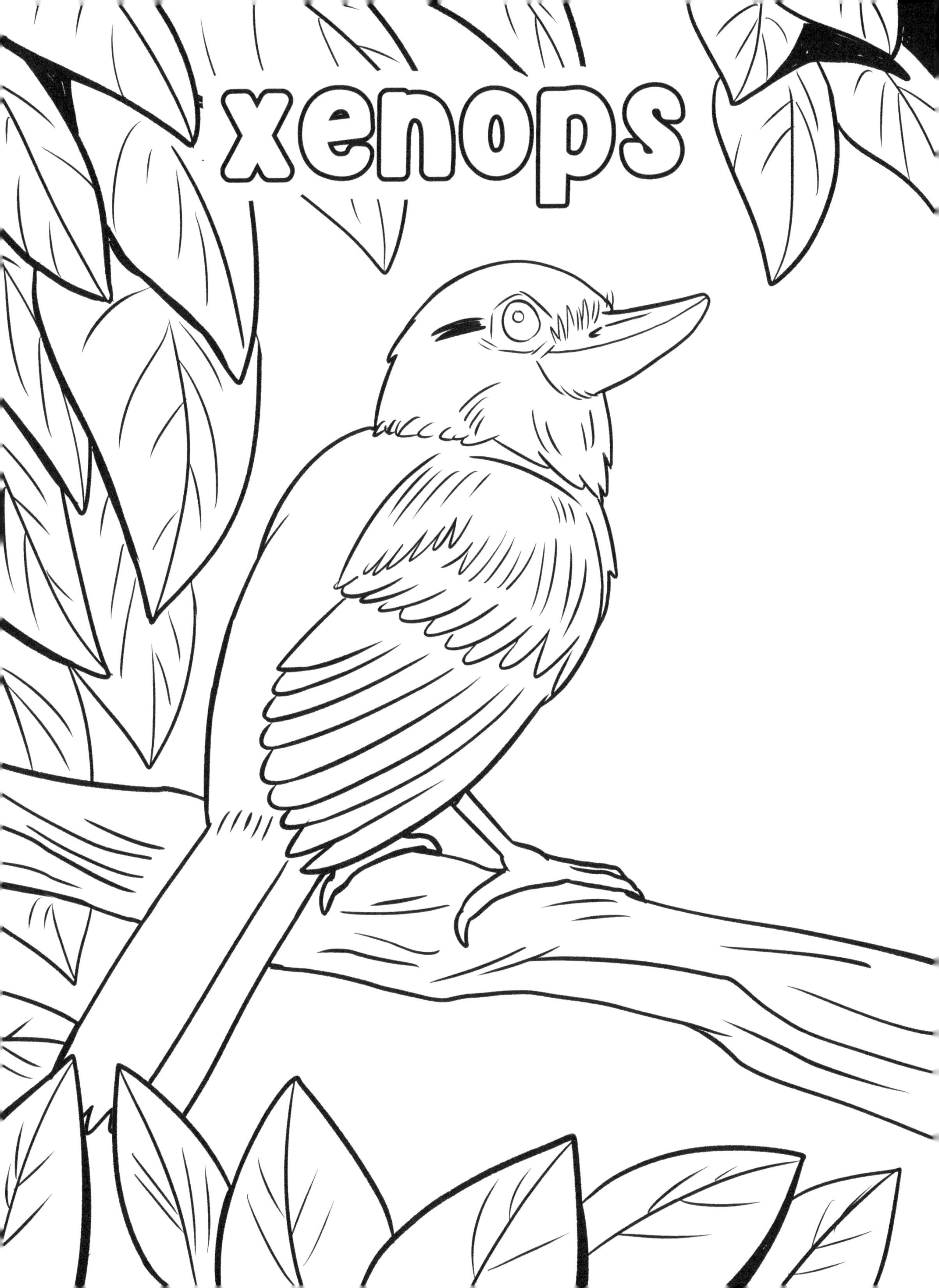
xenops

yellow eyed penguin

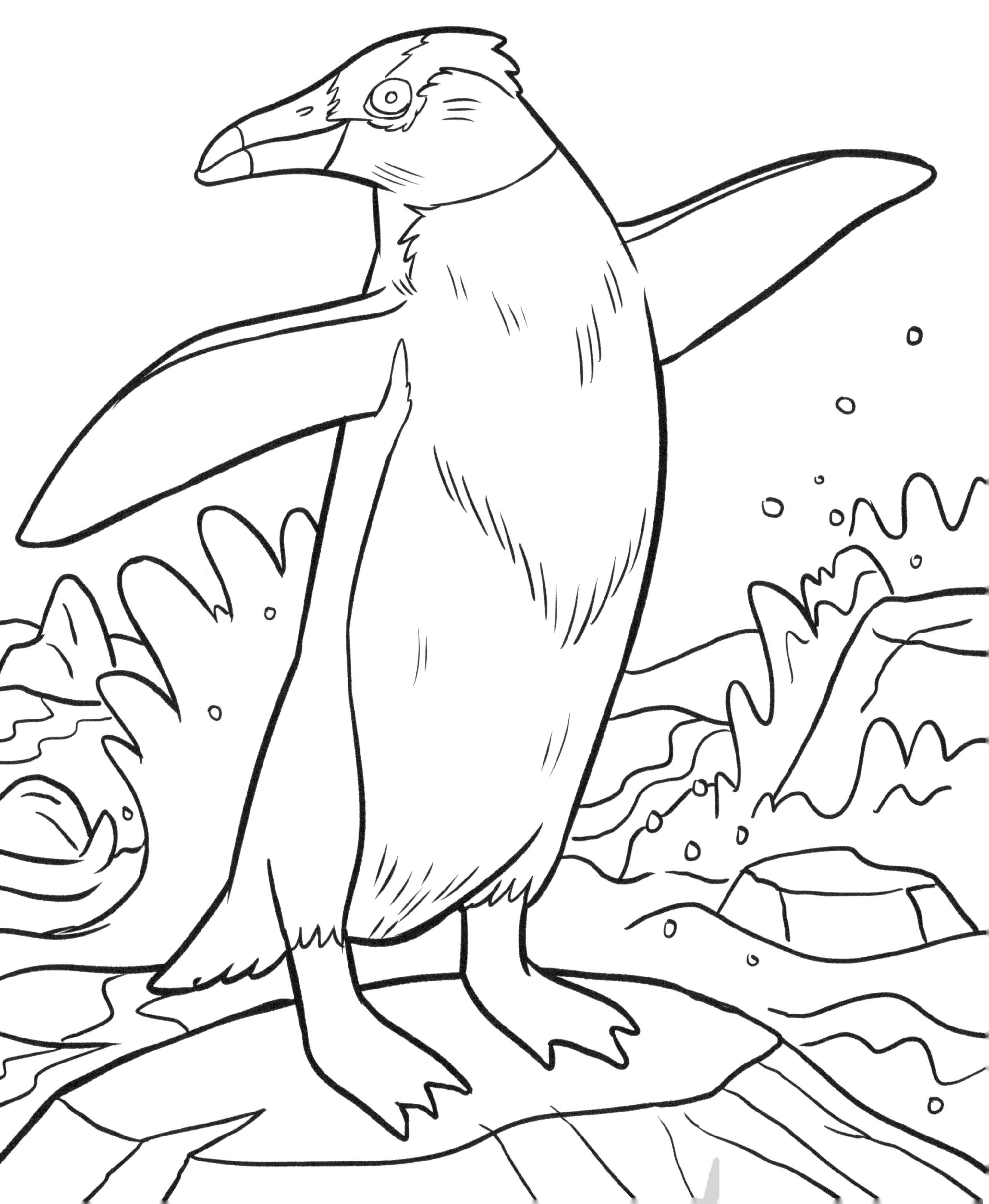

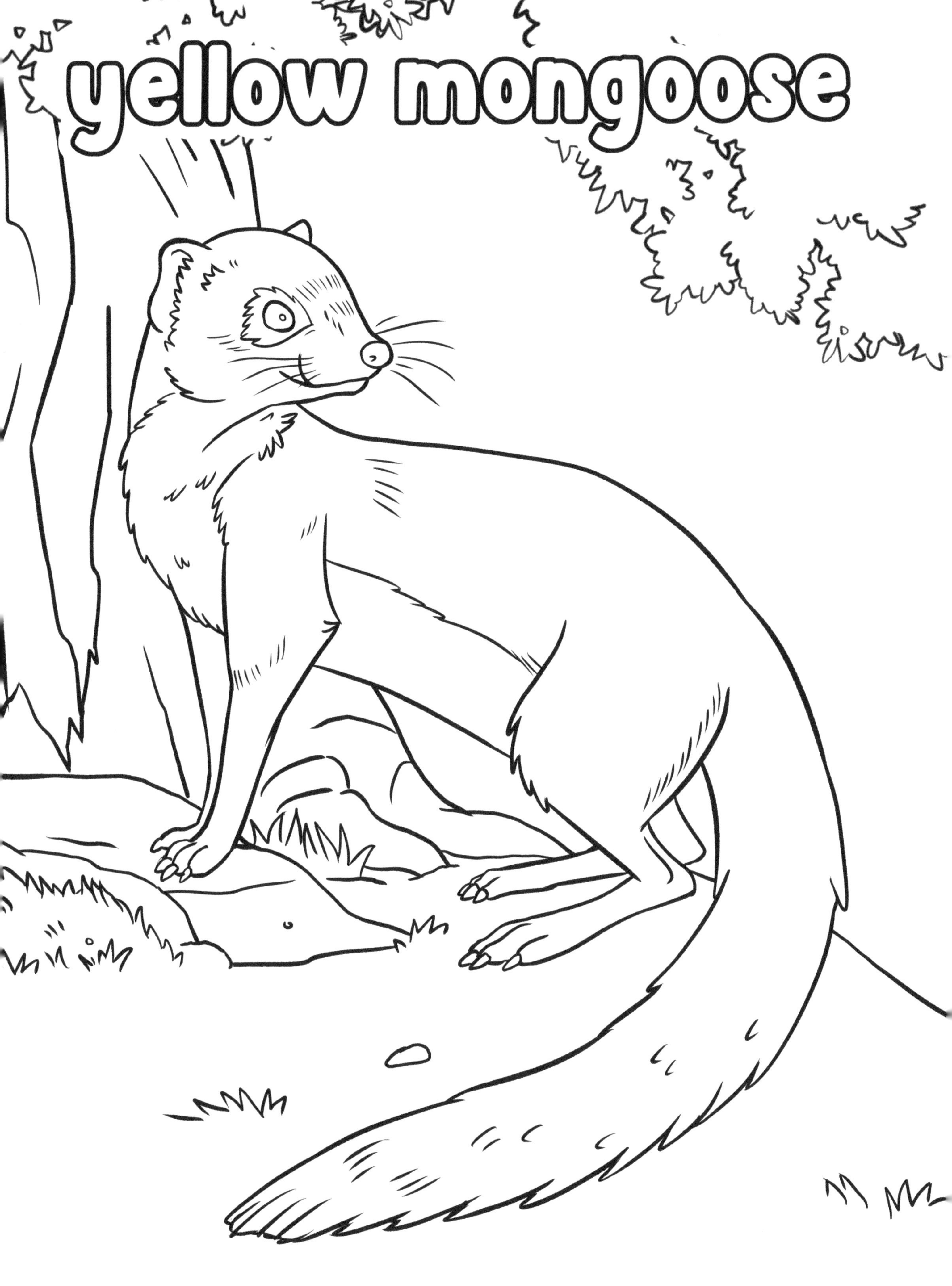
yellow mongoose

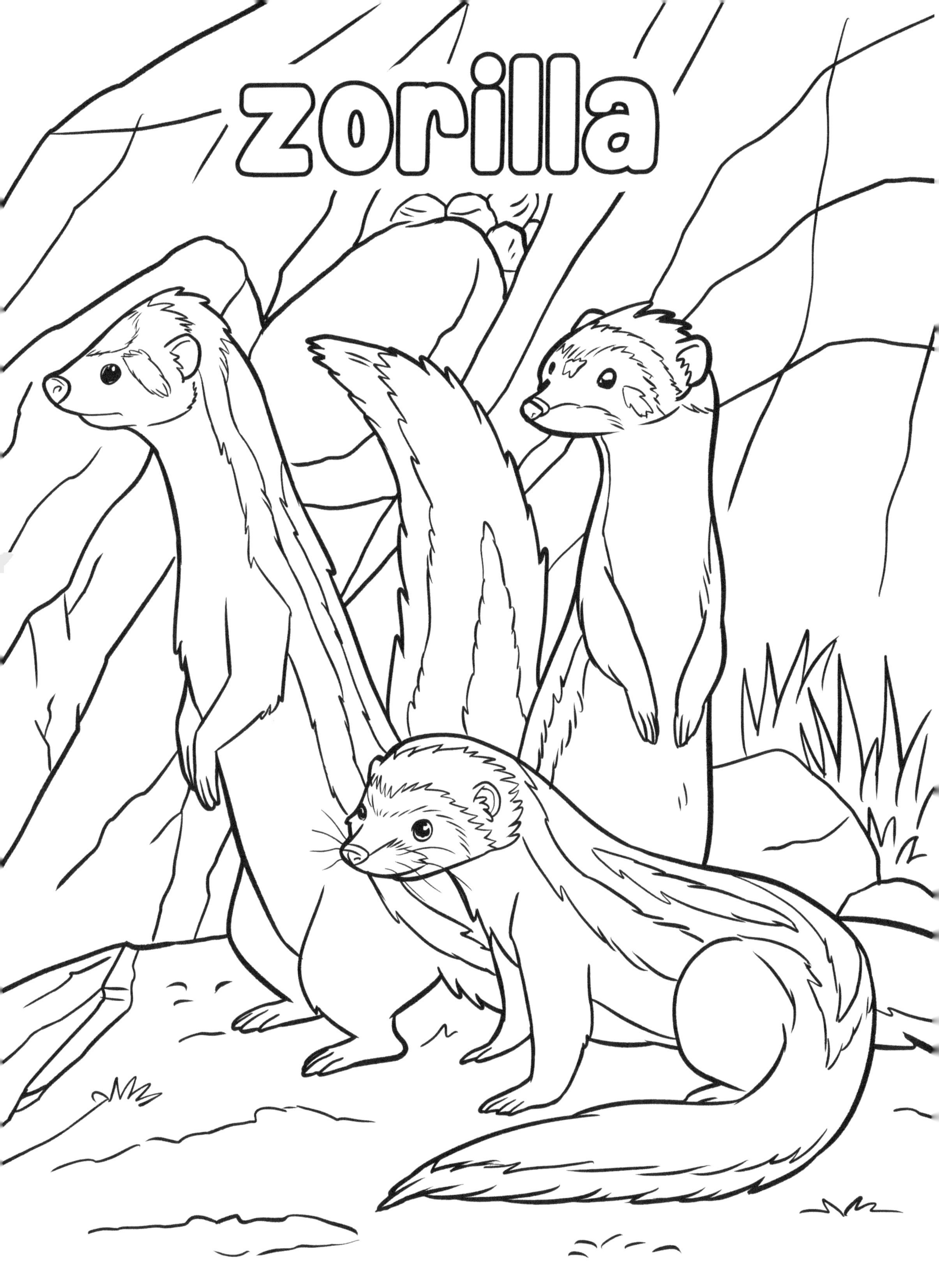
zorilla

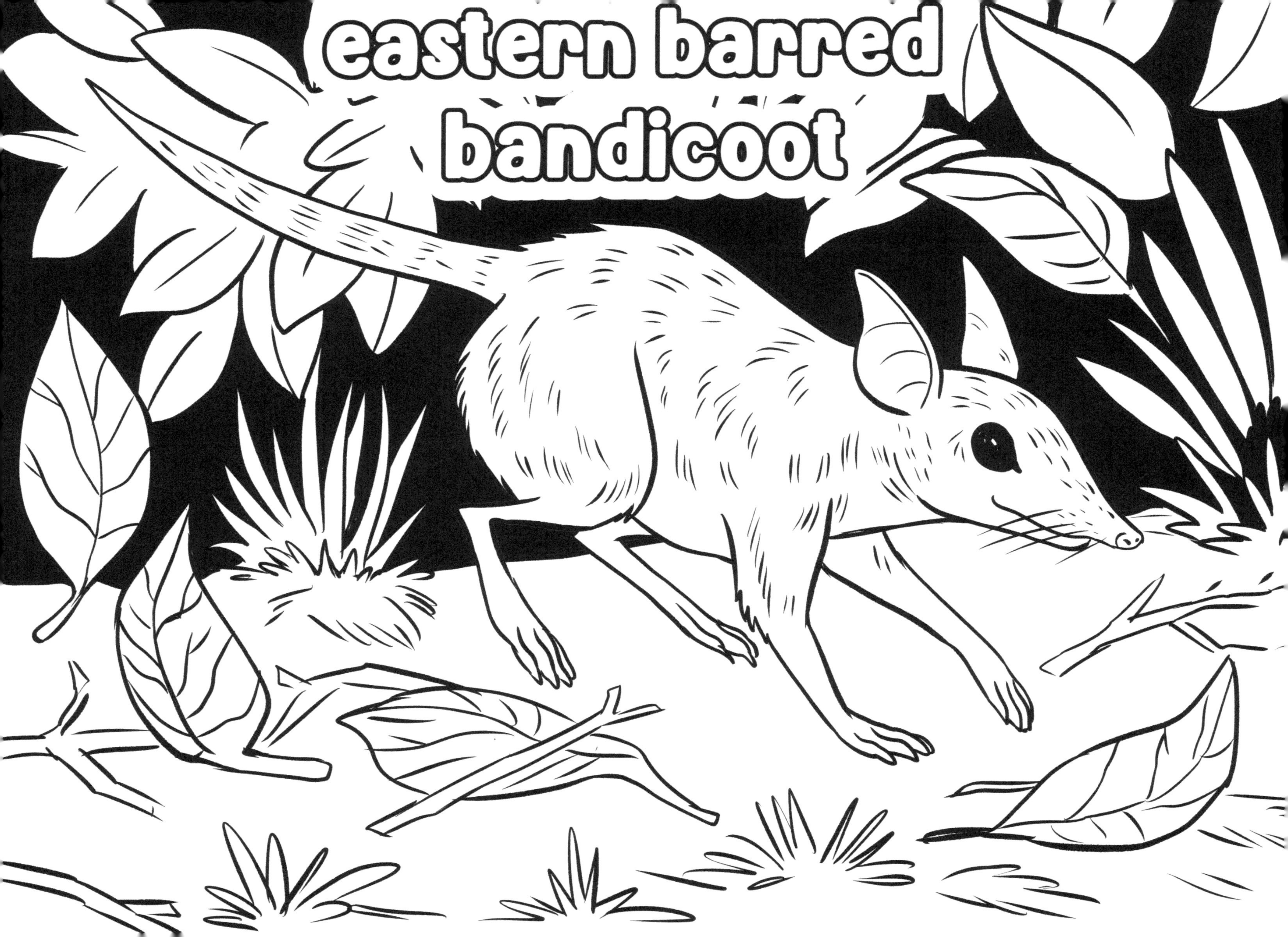
eastern barred
bandicoot

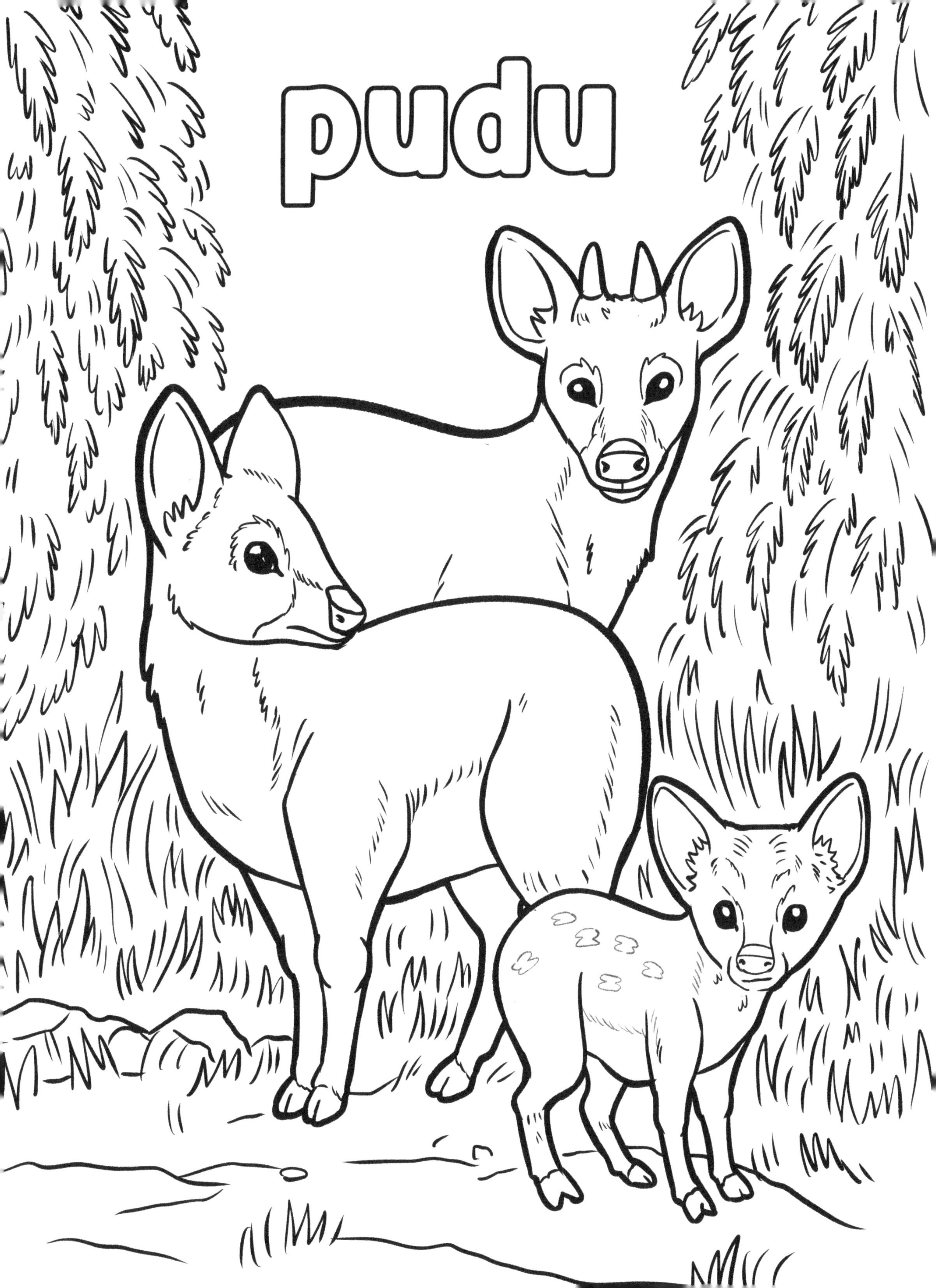
pudu

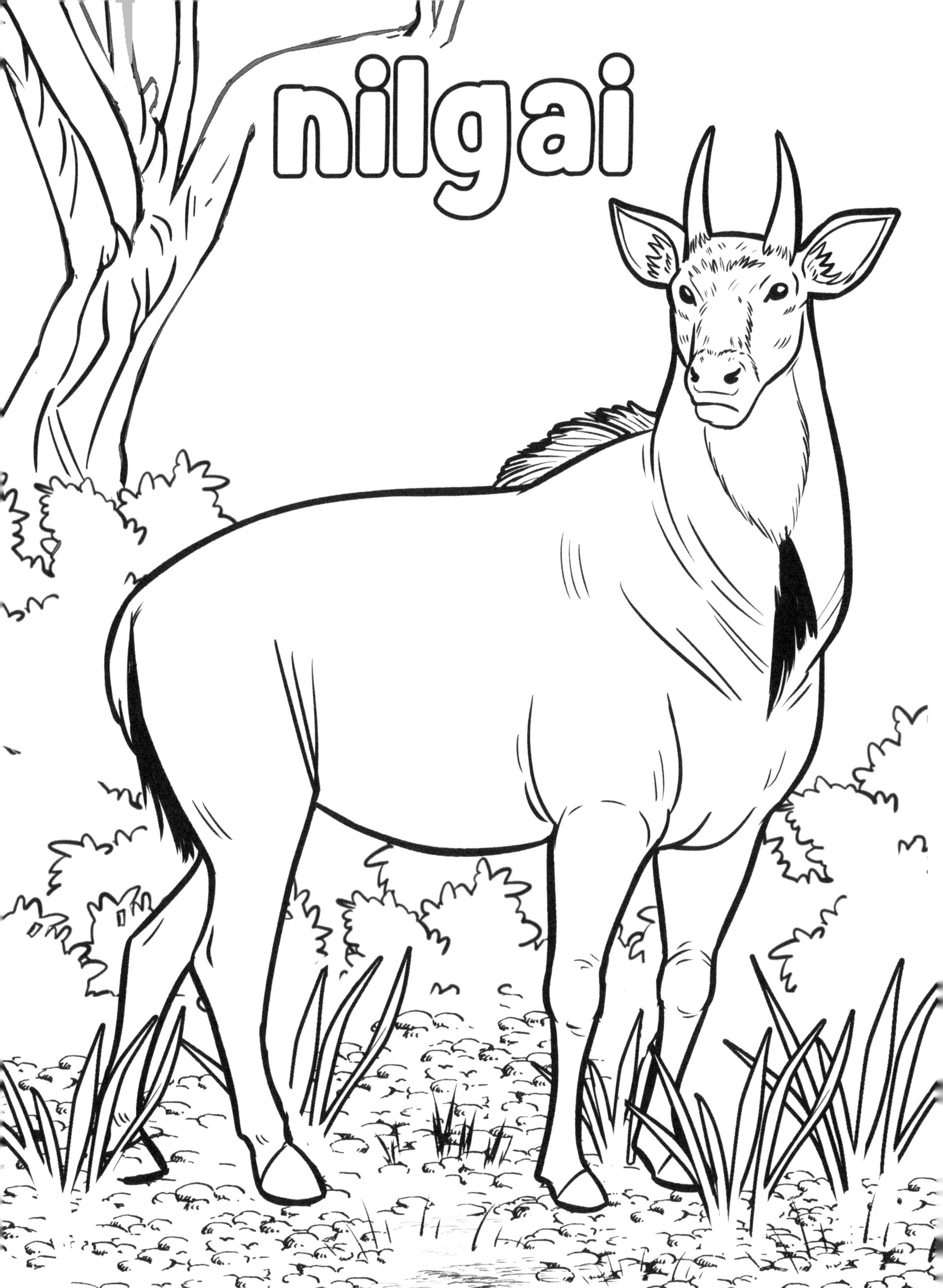
nilgai

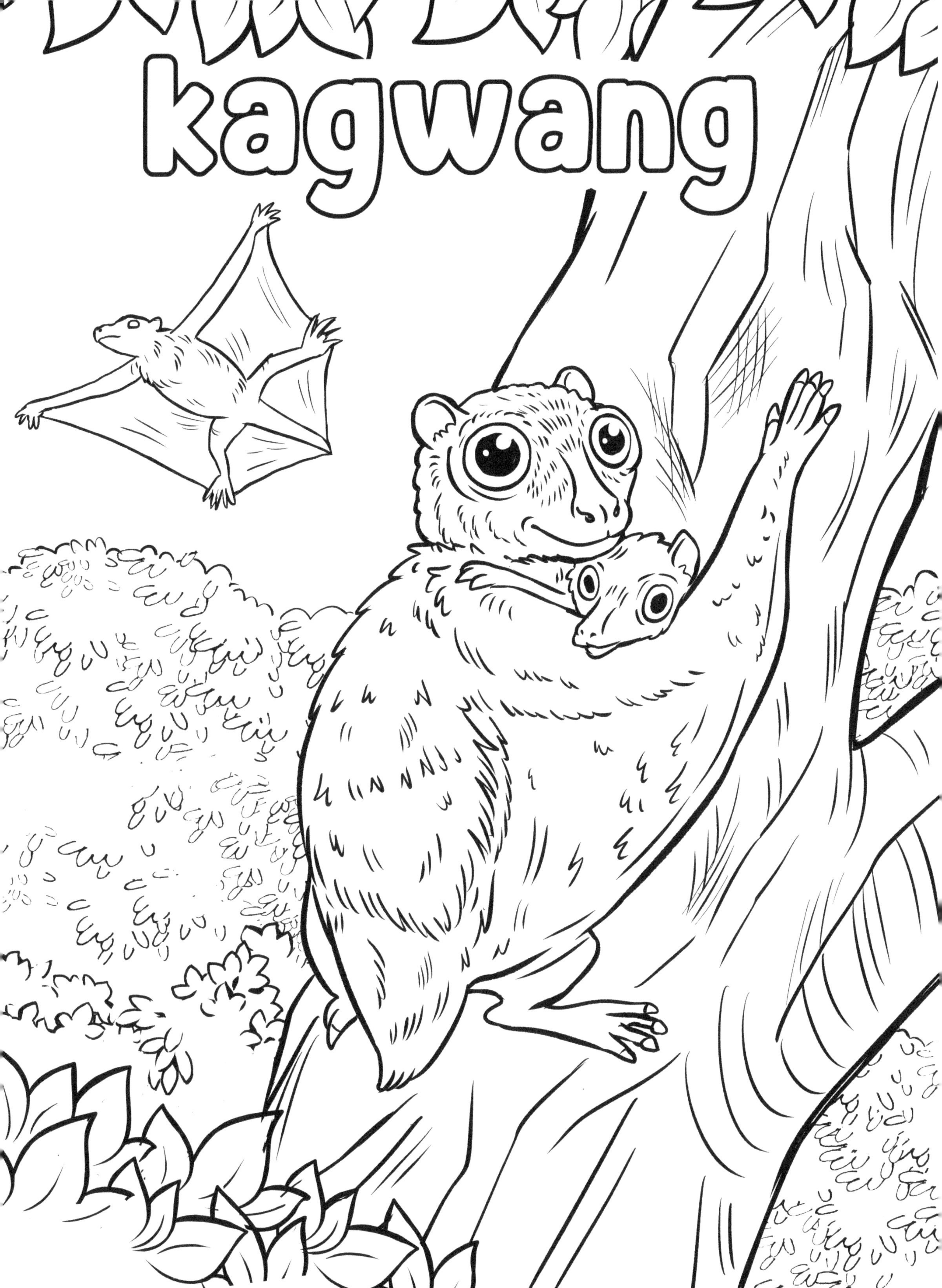
kagwang

maned wolf

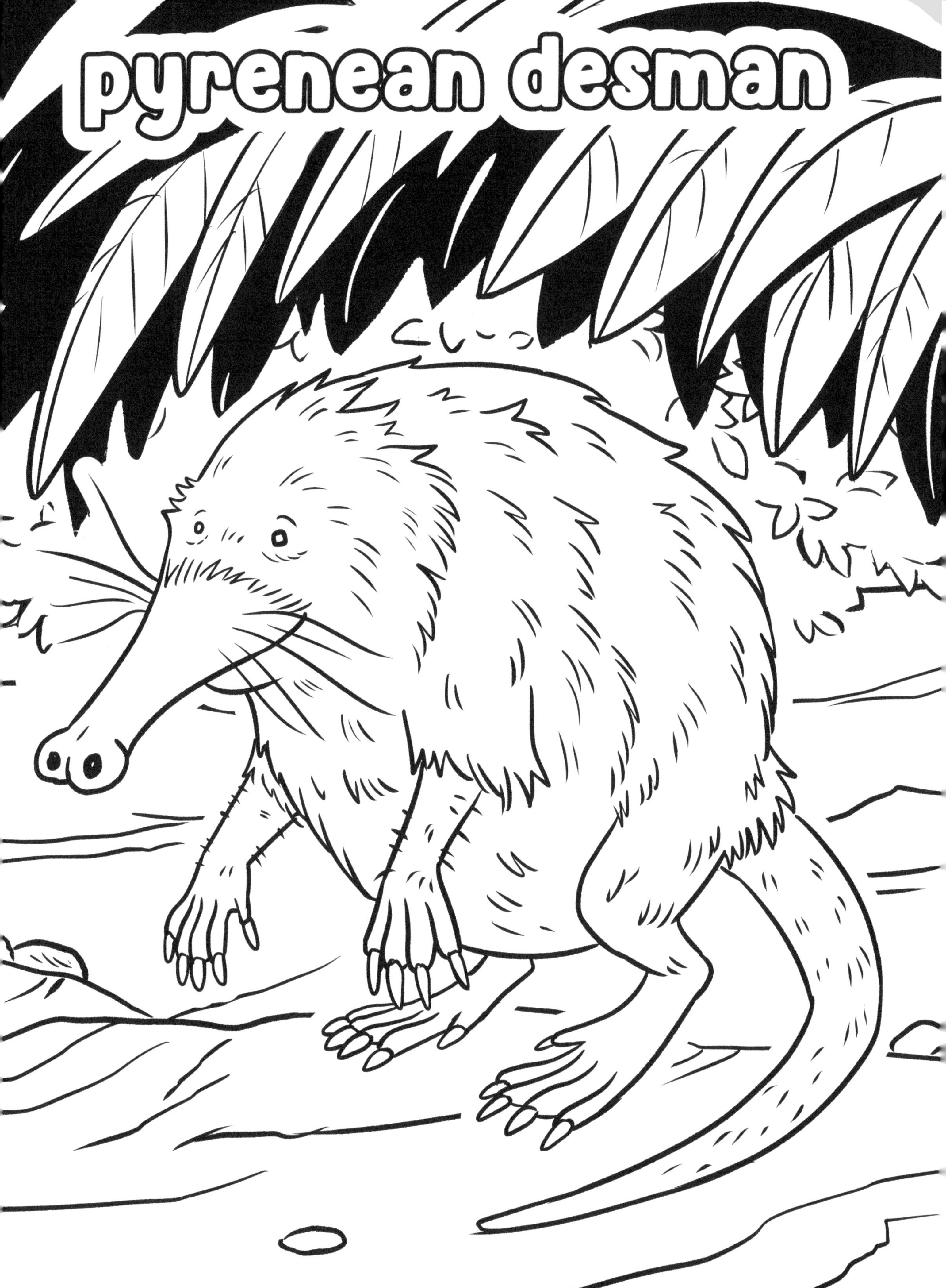
pyrenean desman

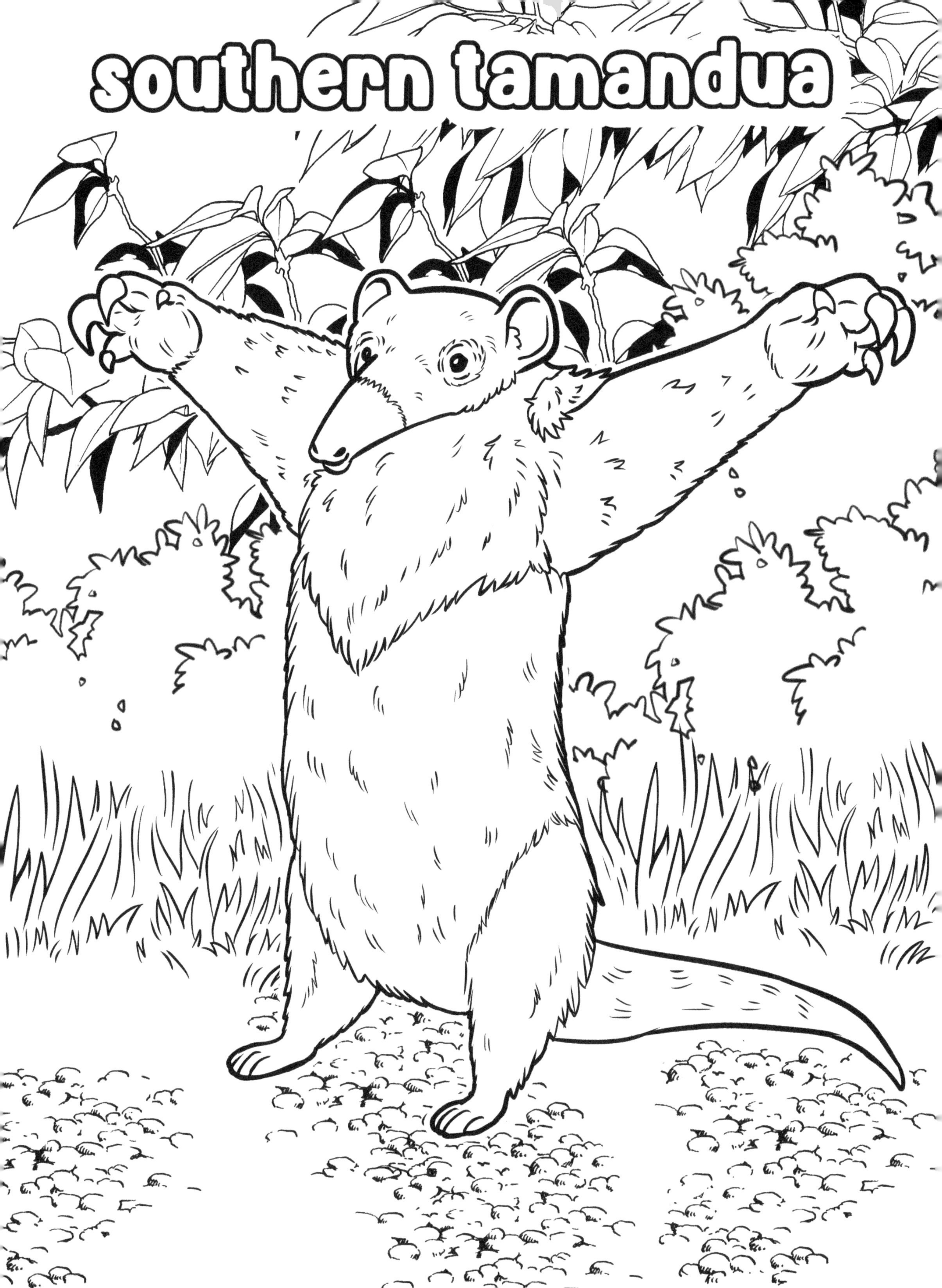
southern tamandua

shoebill stork

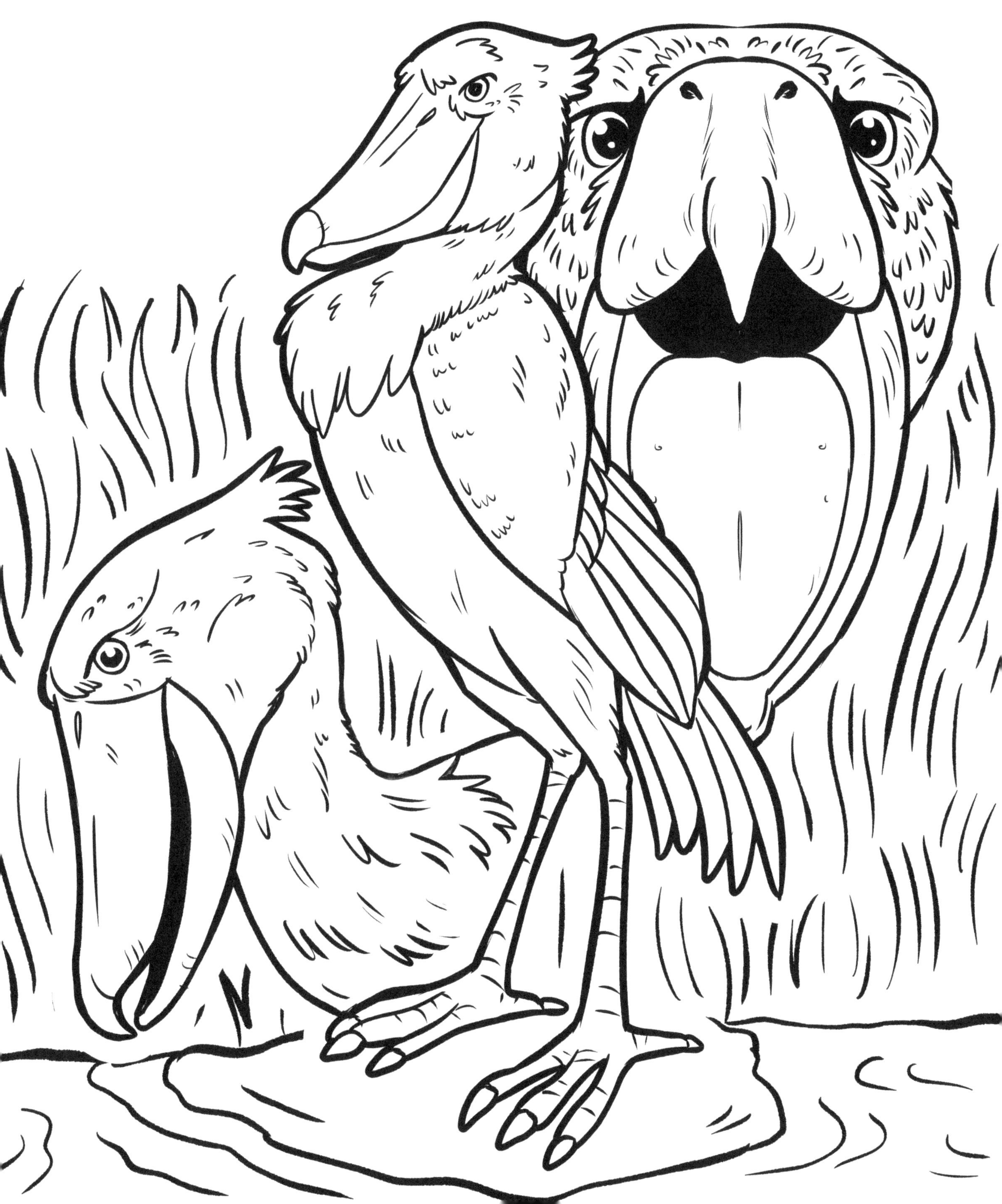

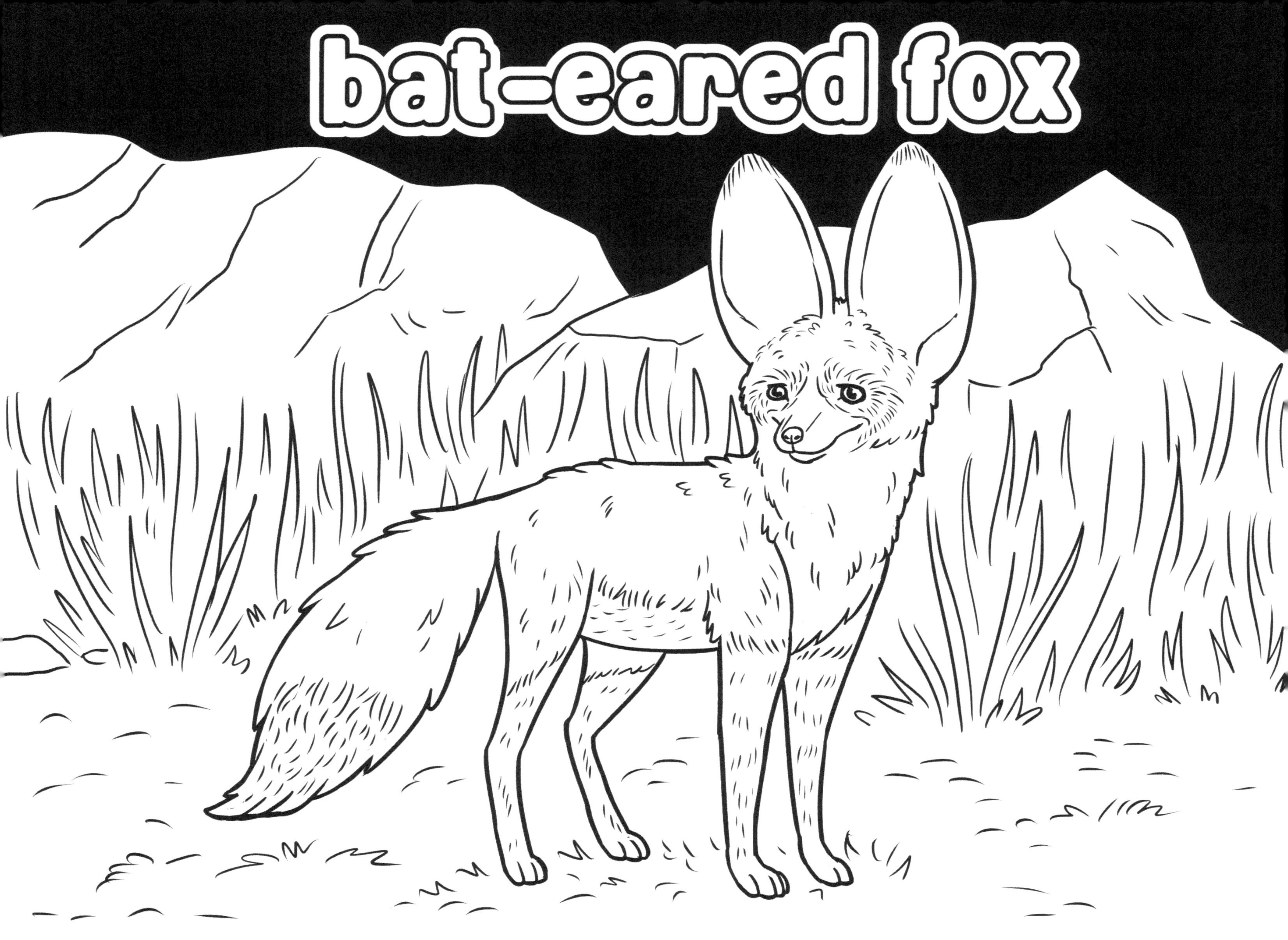
bat-eared fox

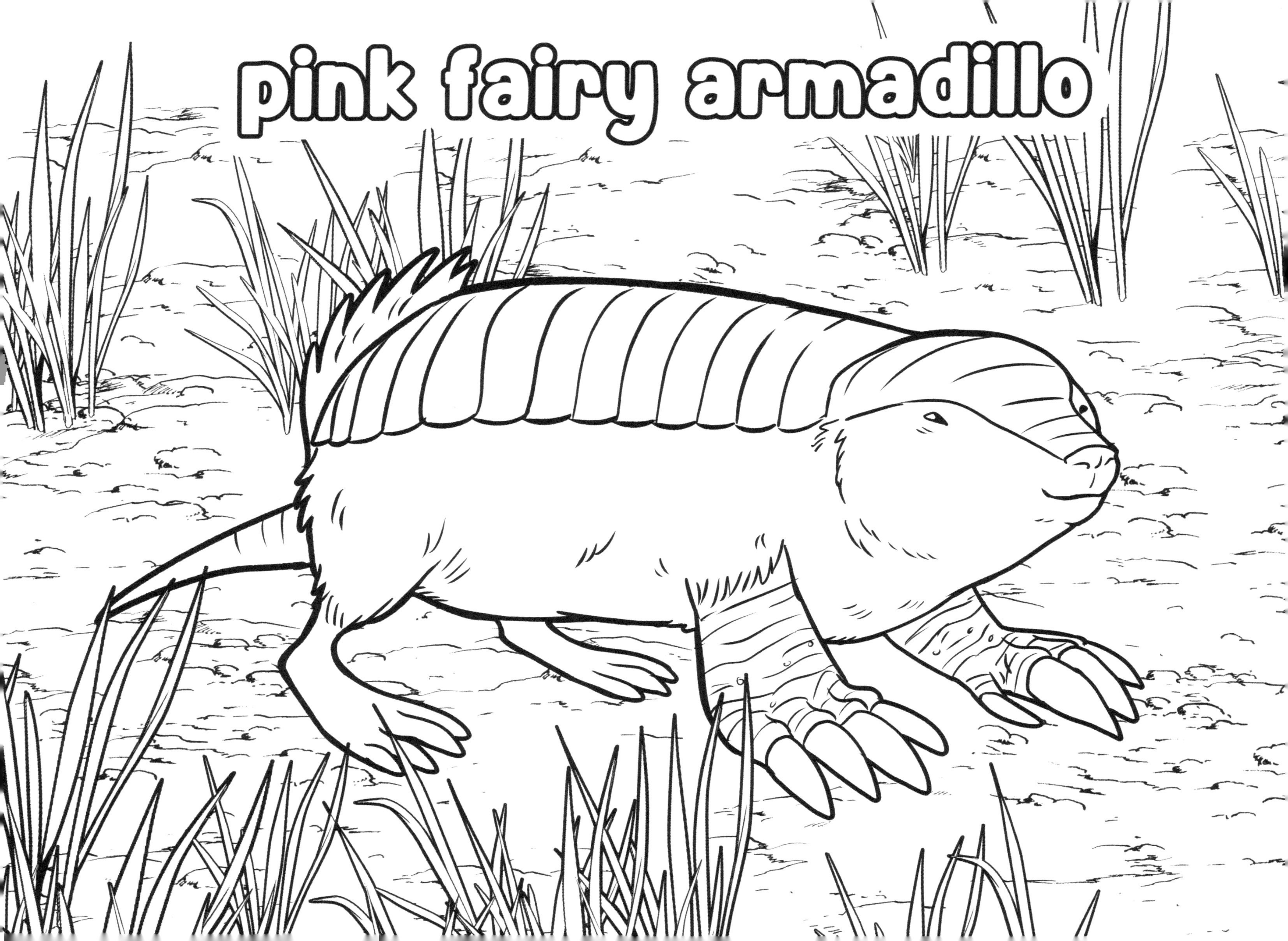
pink fairy armadillo

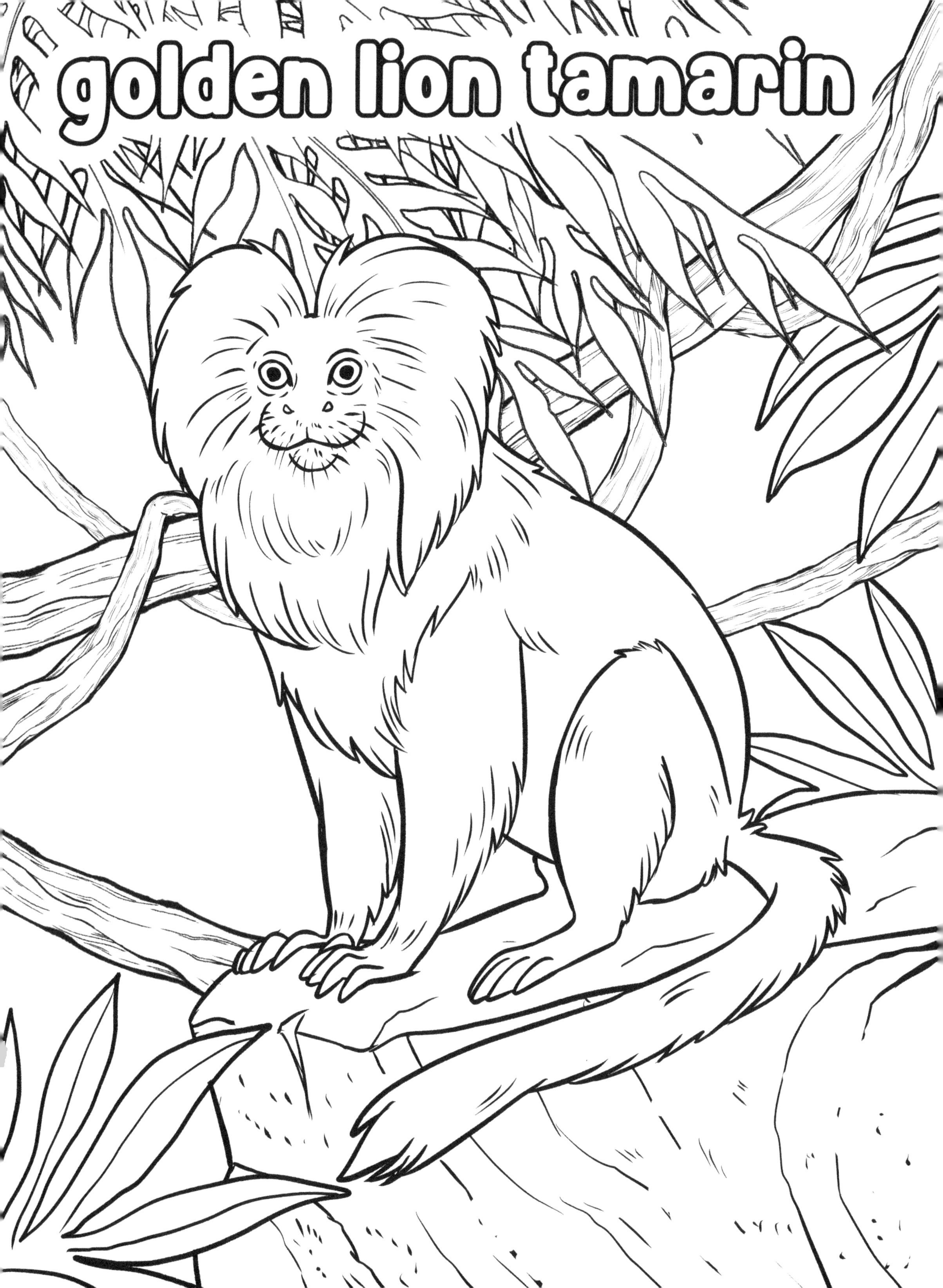
golden lion tamarin

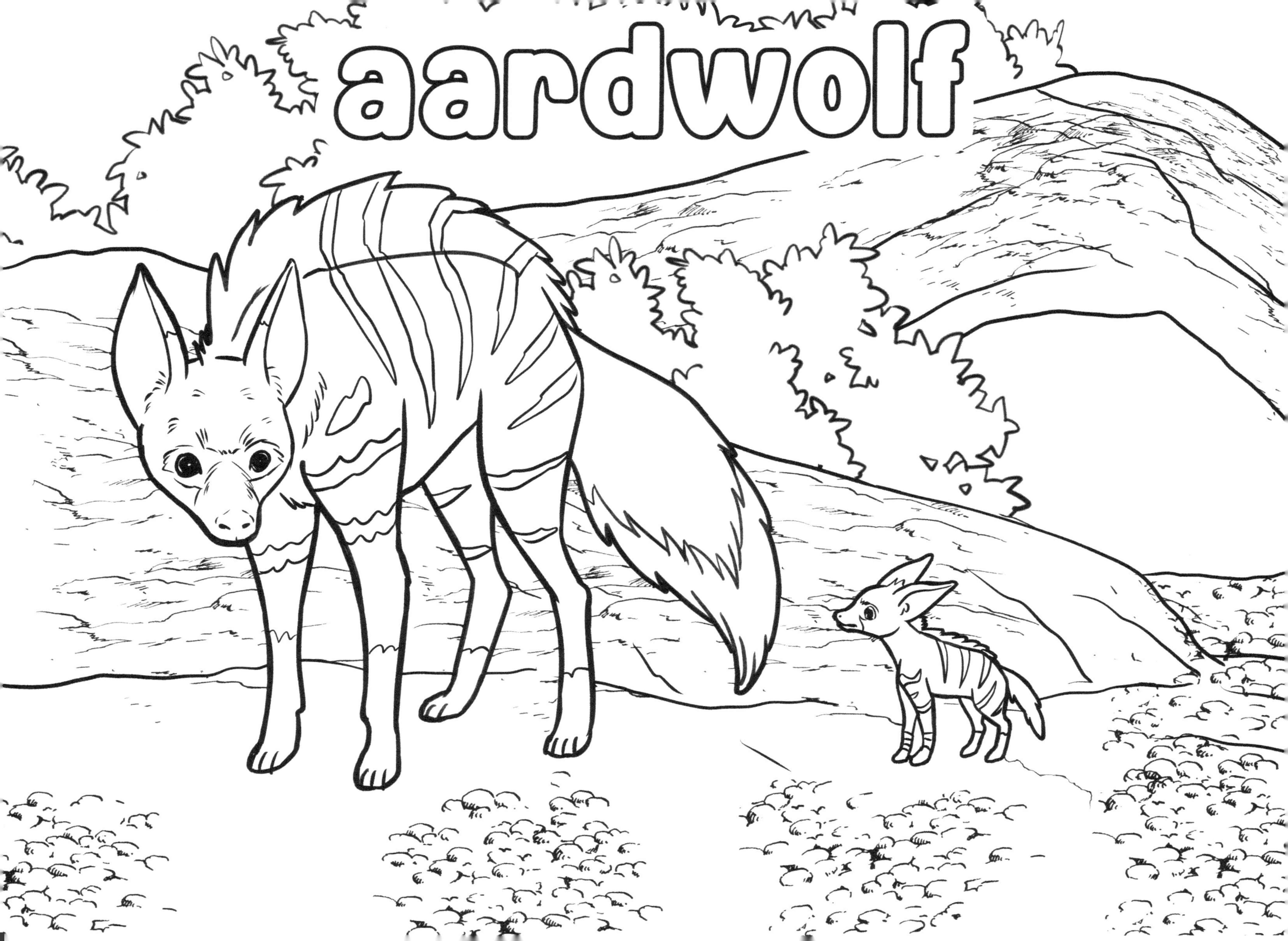
aardwolf

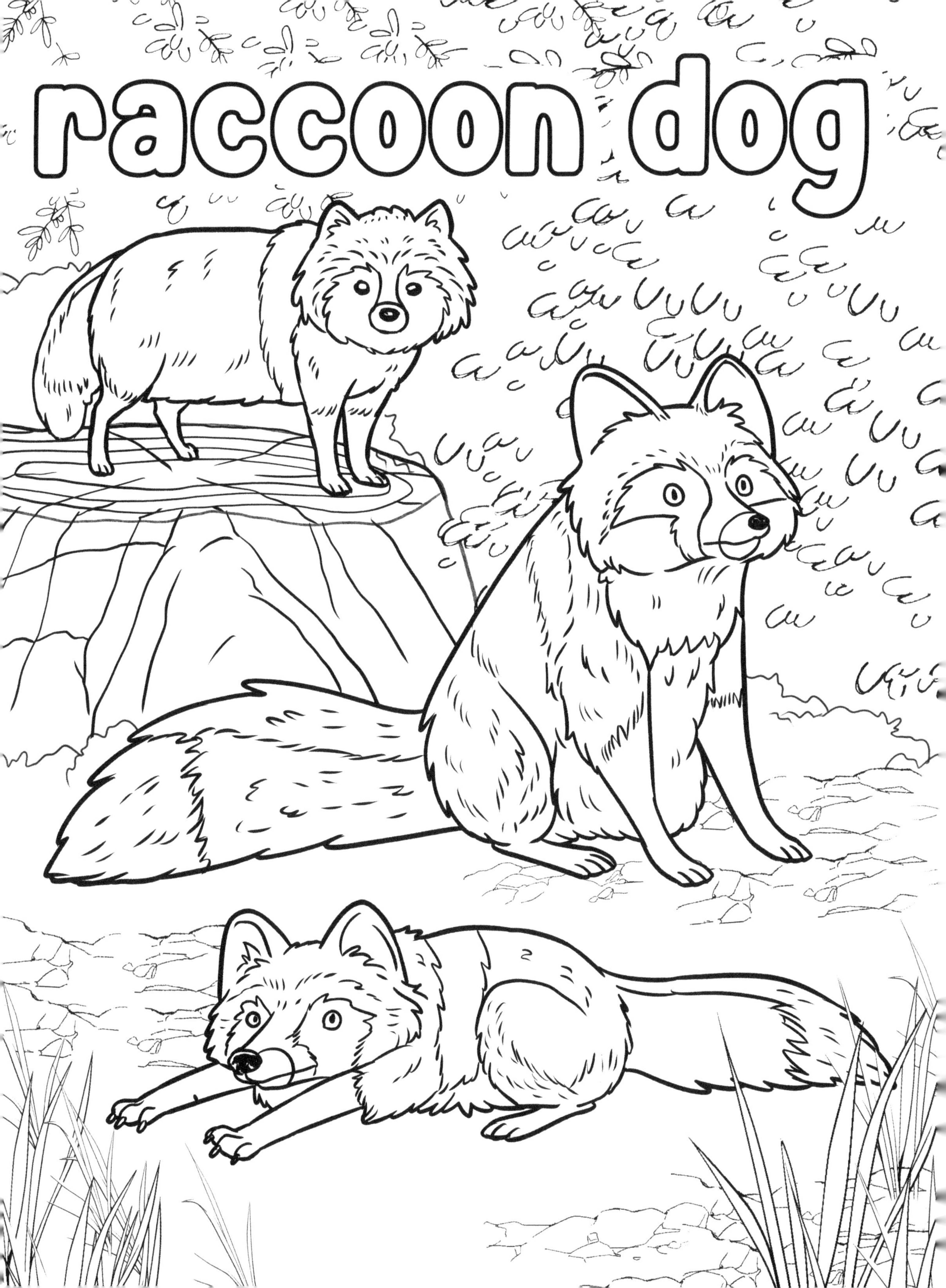
raccoon dog

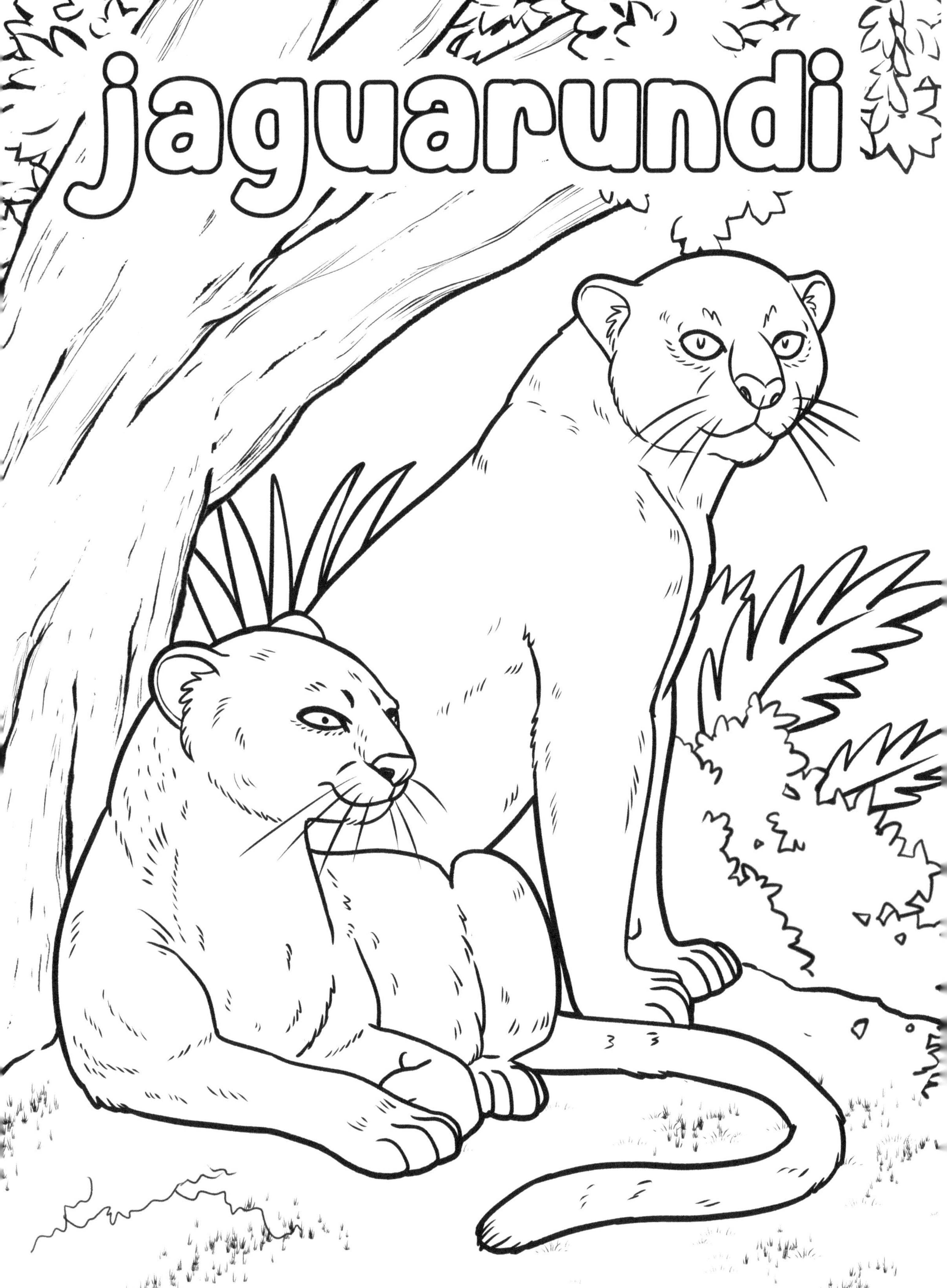
jaguarundi

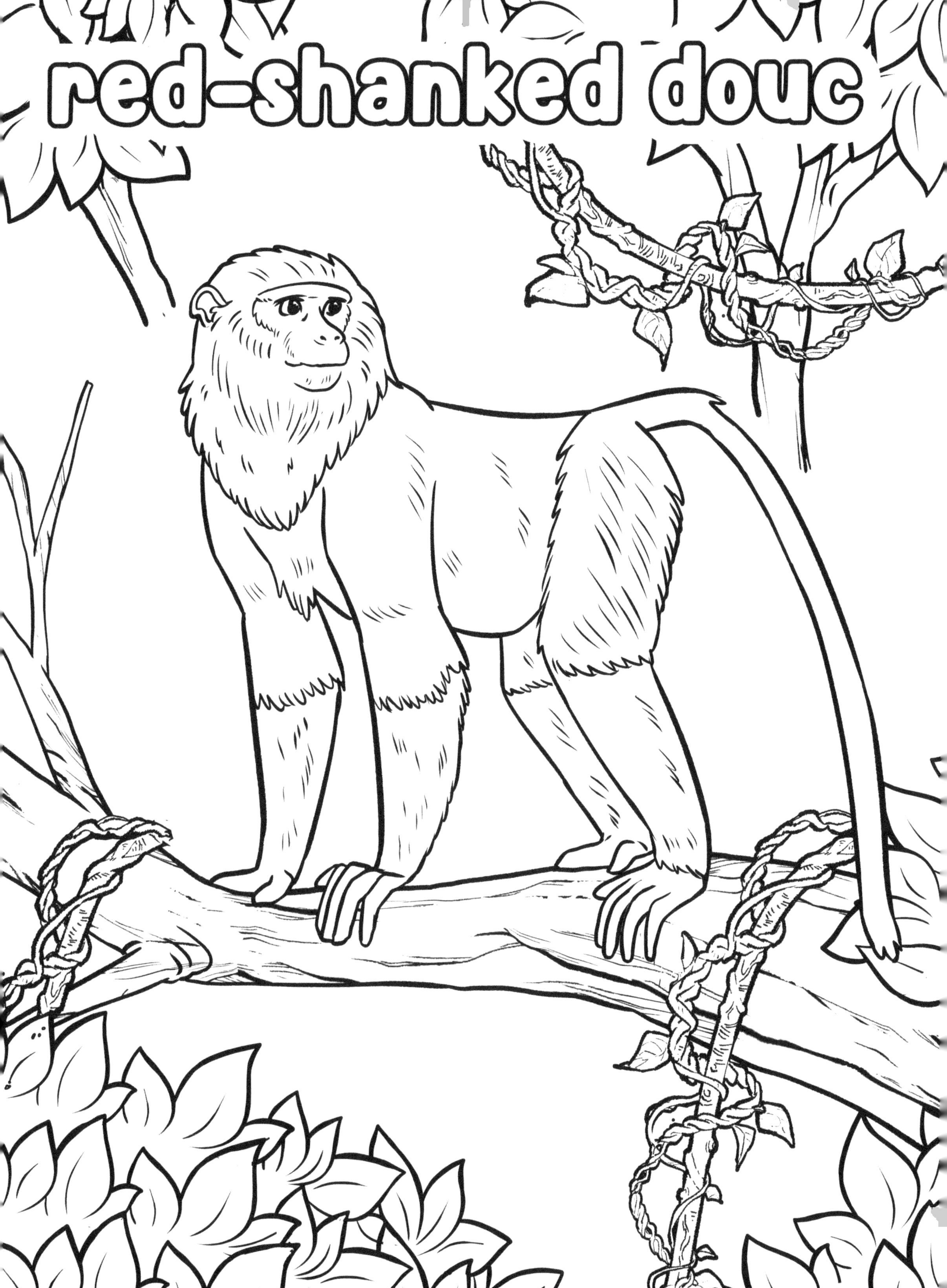
red-shanked douc

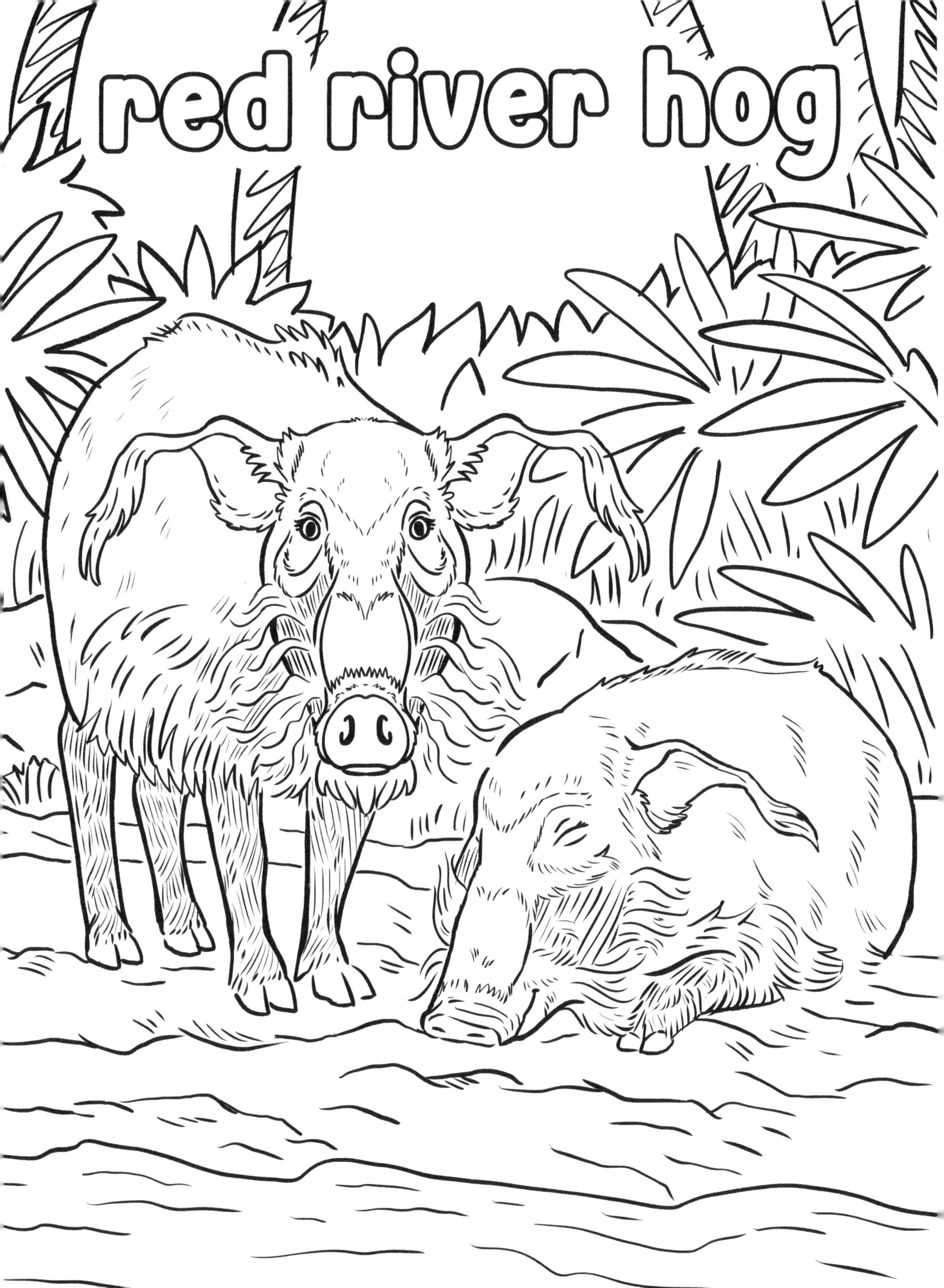
red river hog

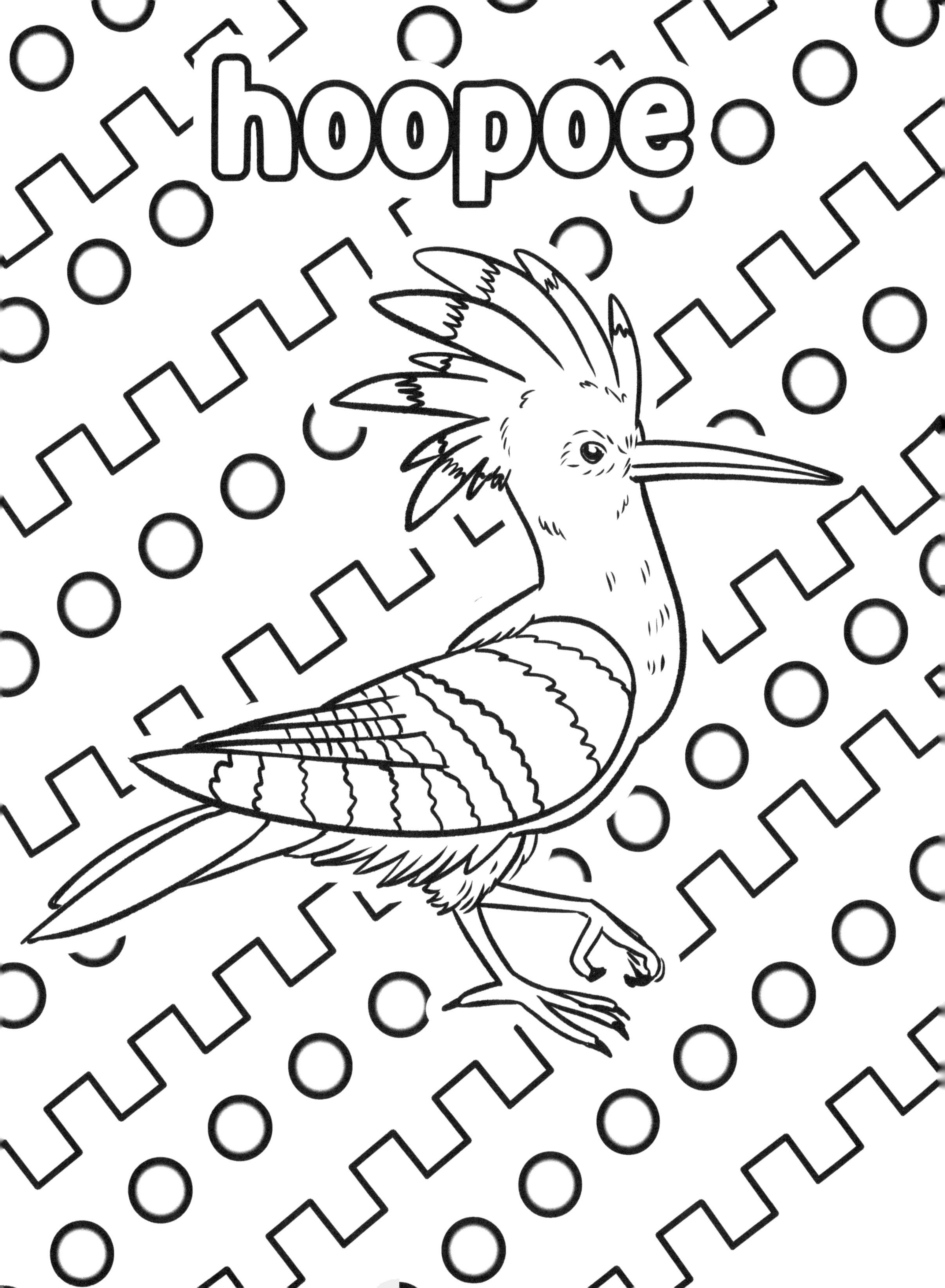
hoopoe

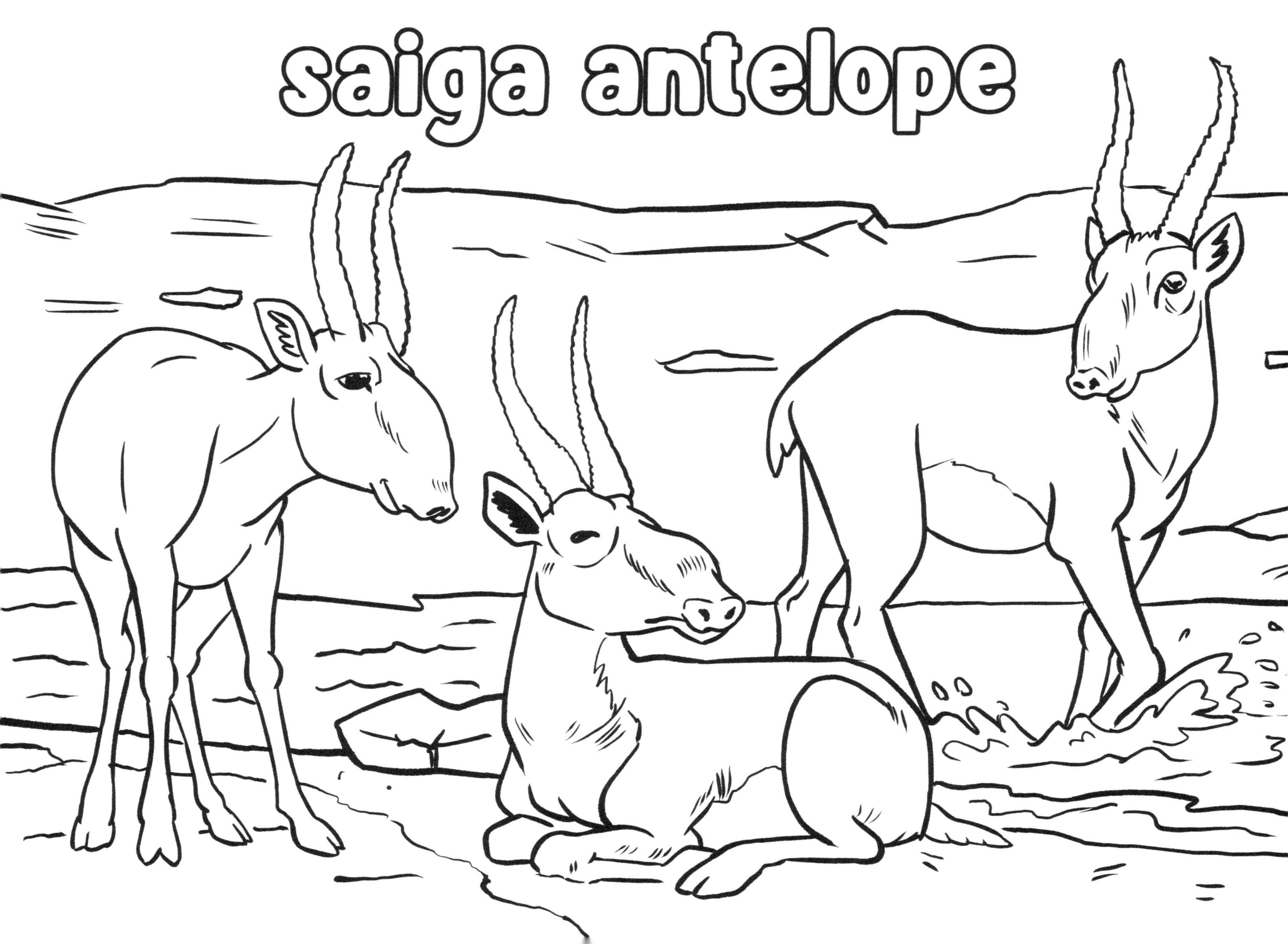
saiga antelope

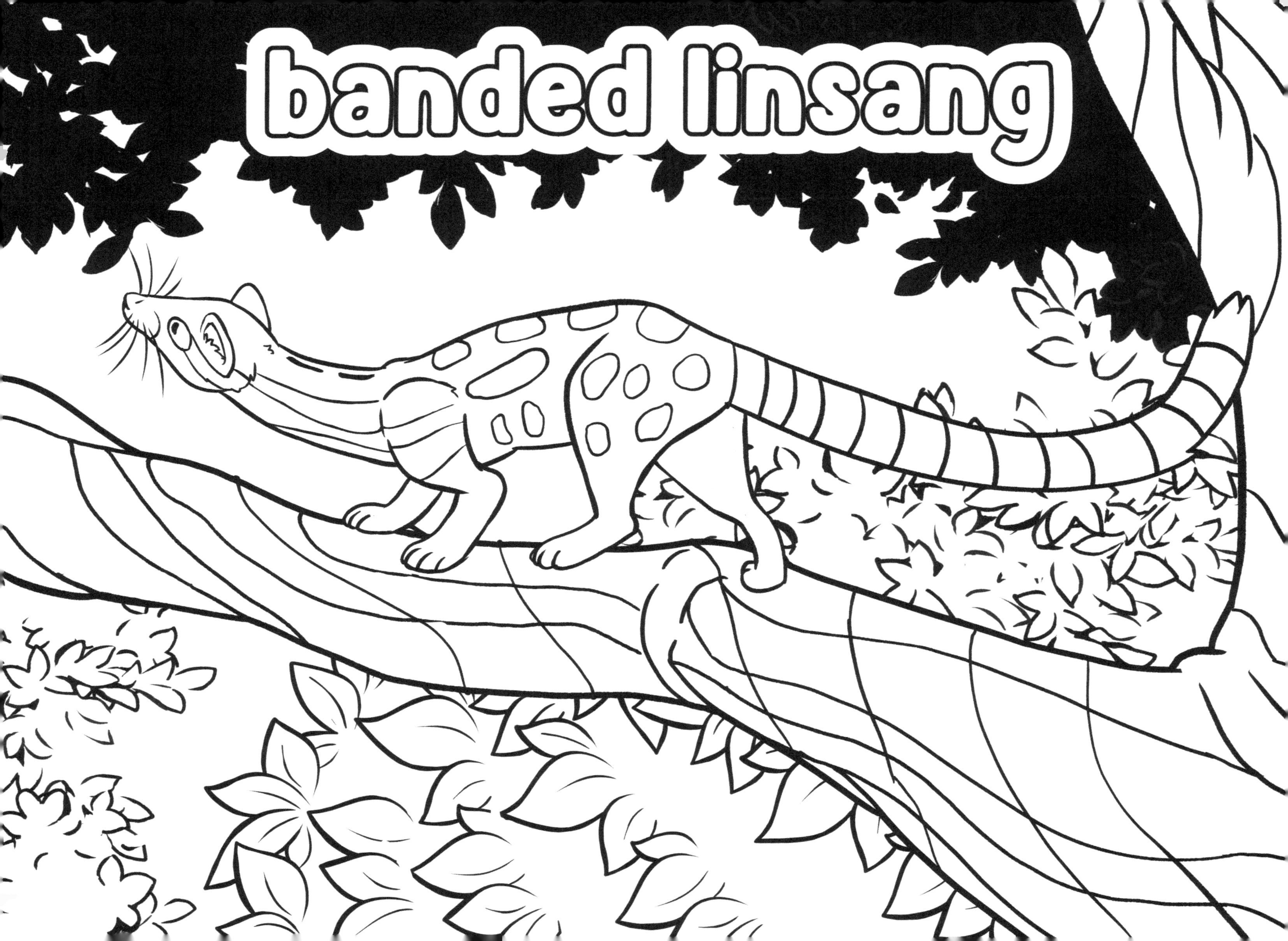
banded linsang

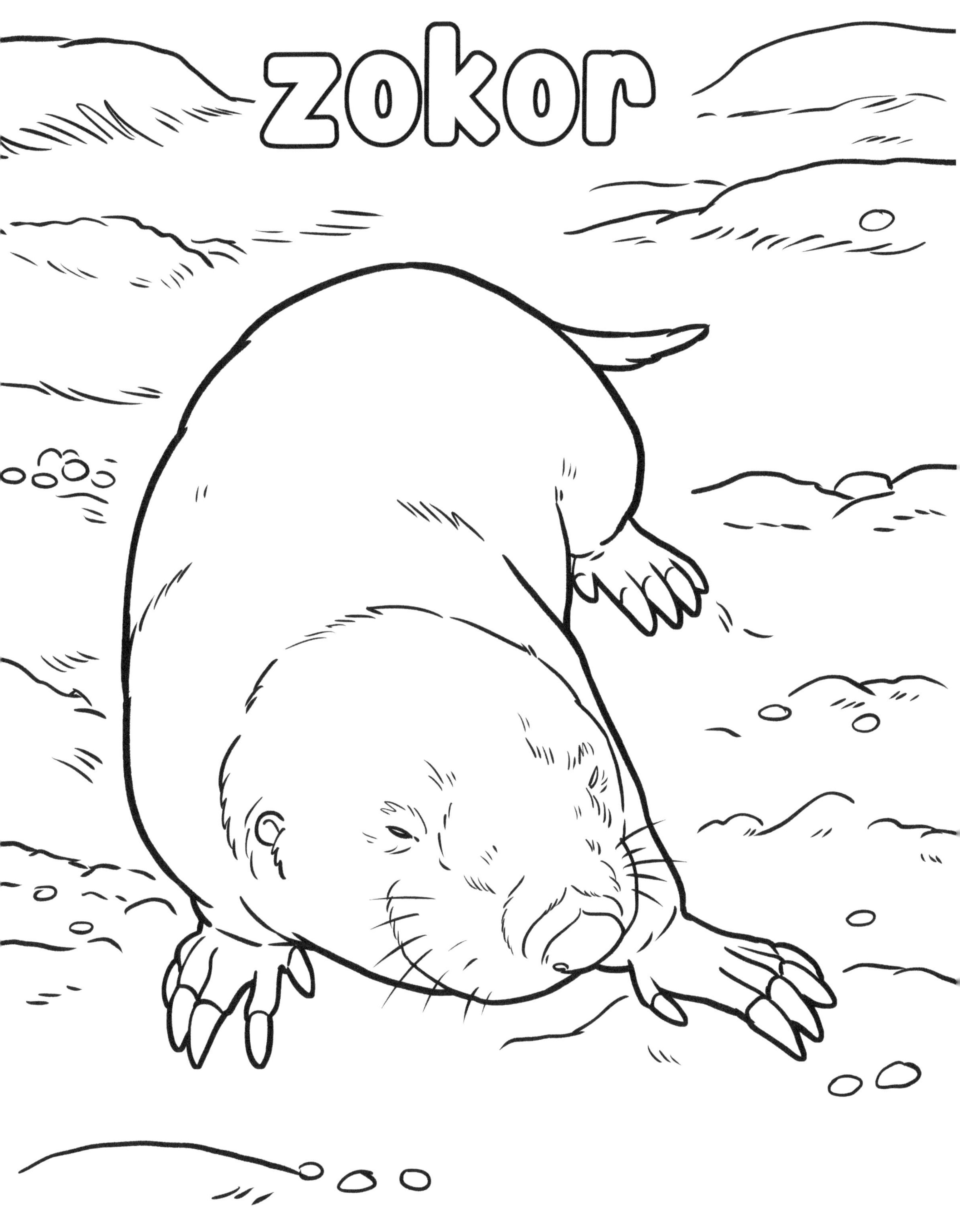
zokor

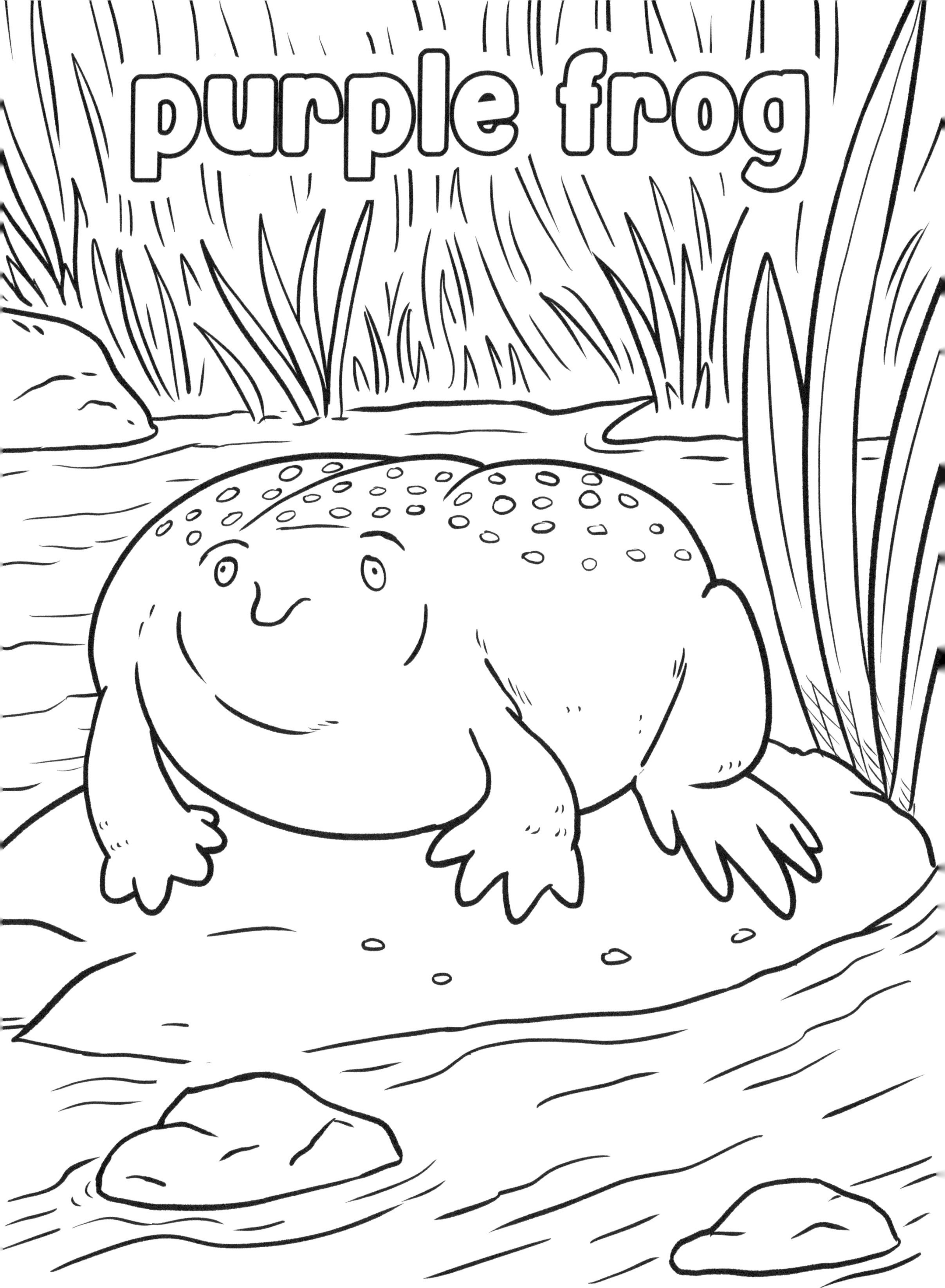
purple frog

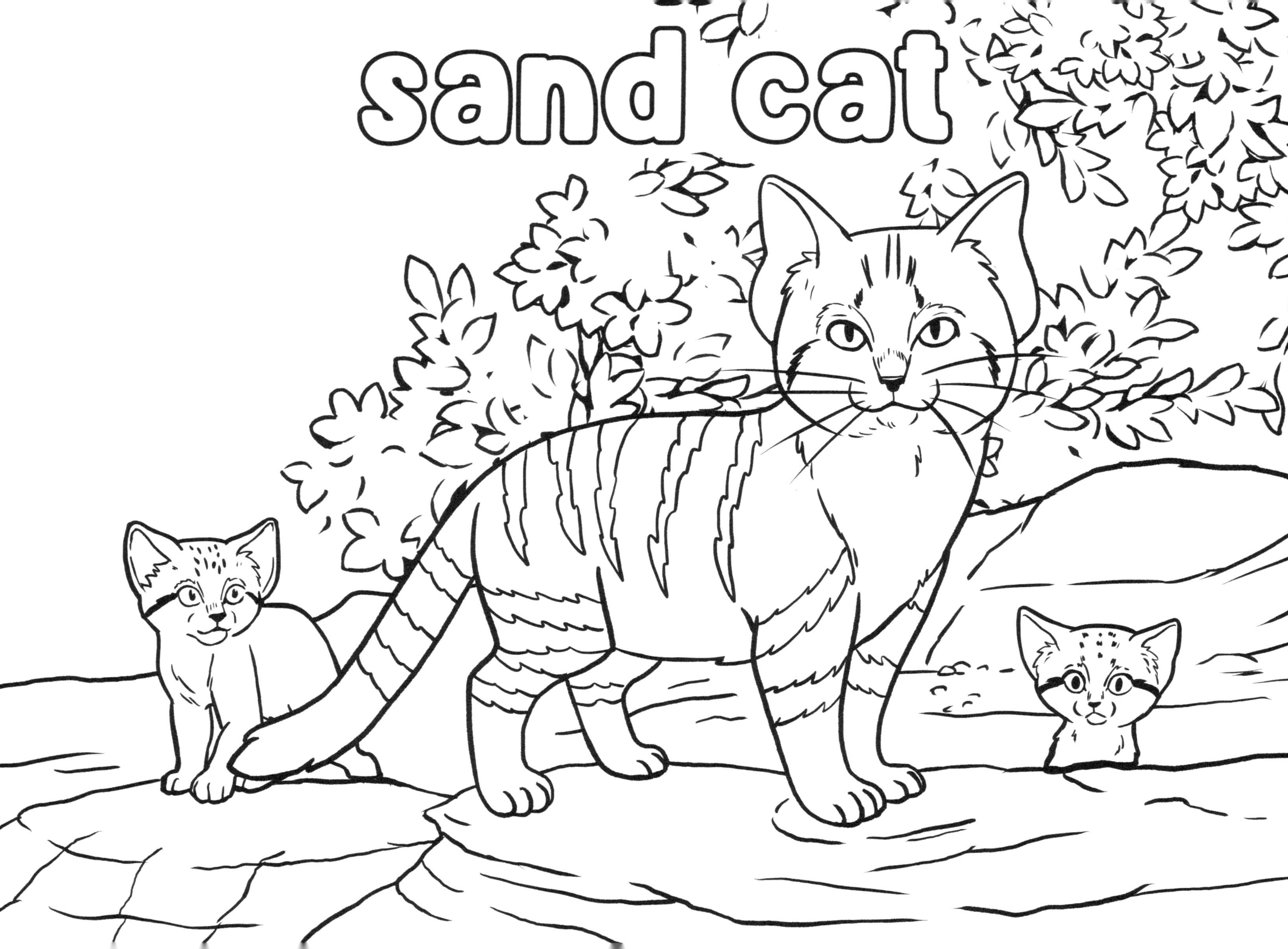
sand cat

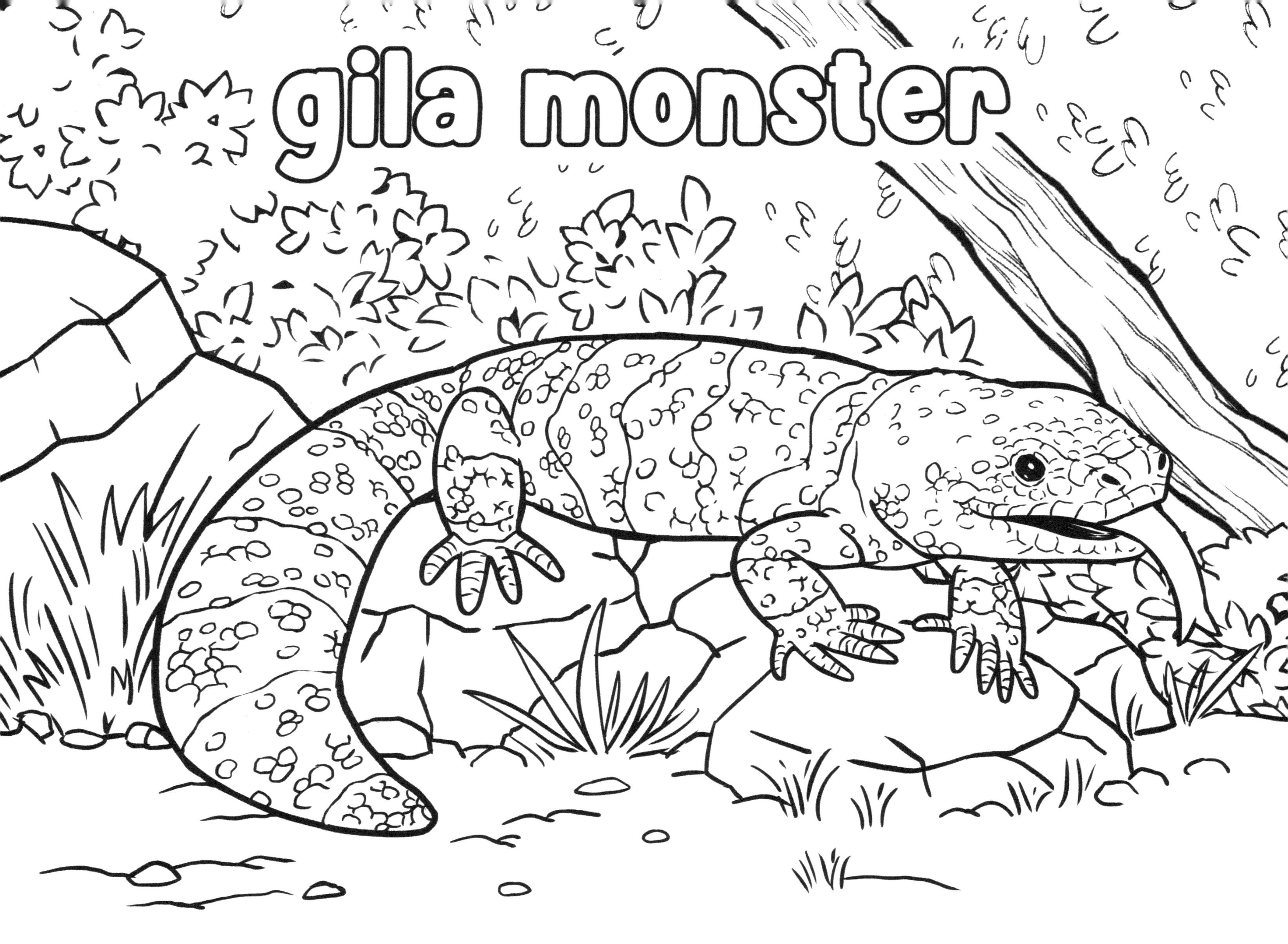
gila monster

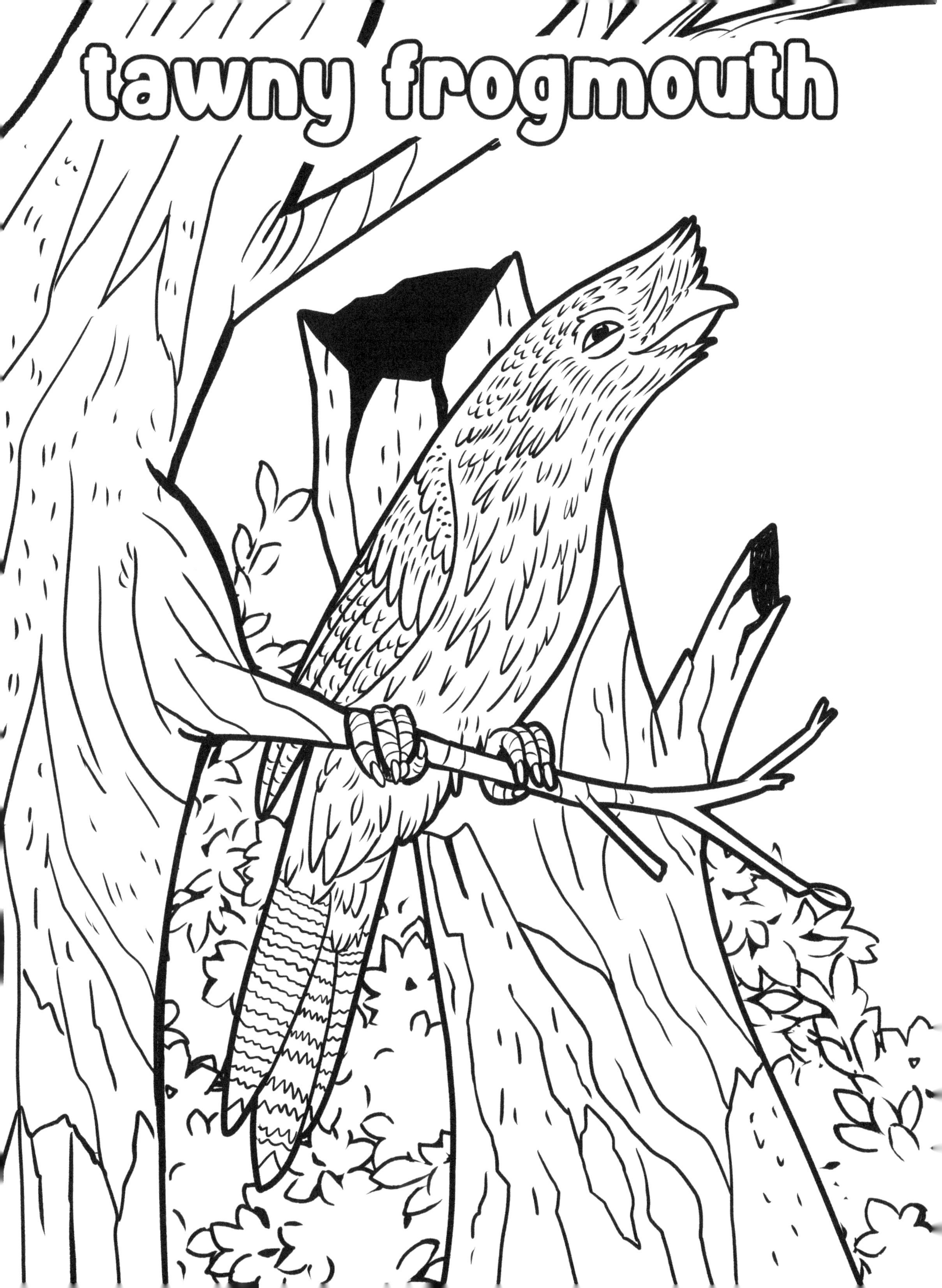
tawny frogmouth

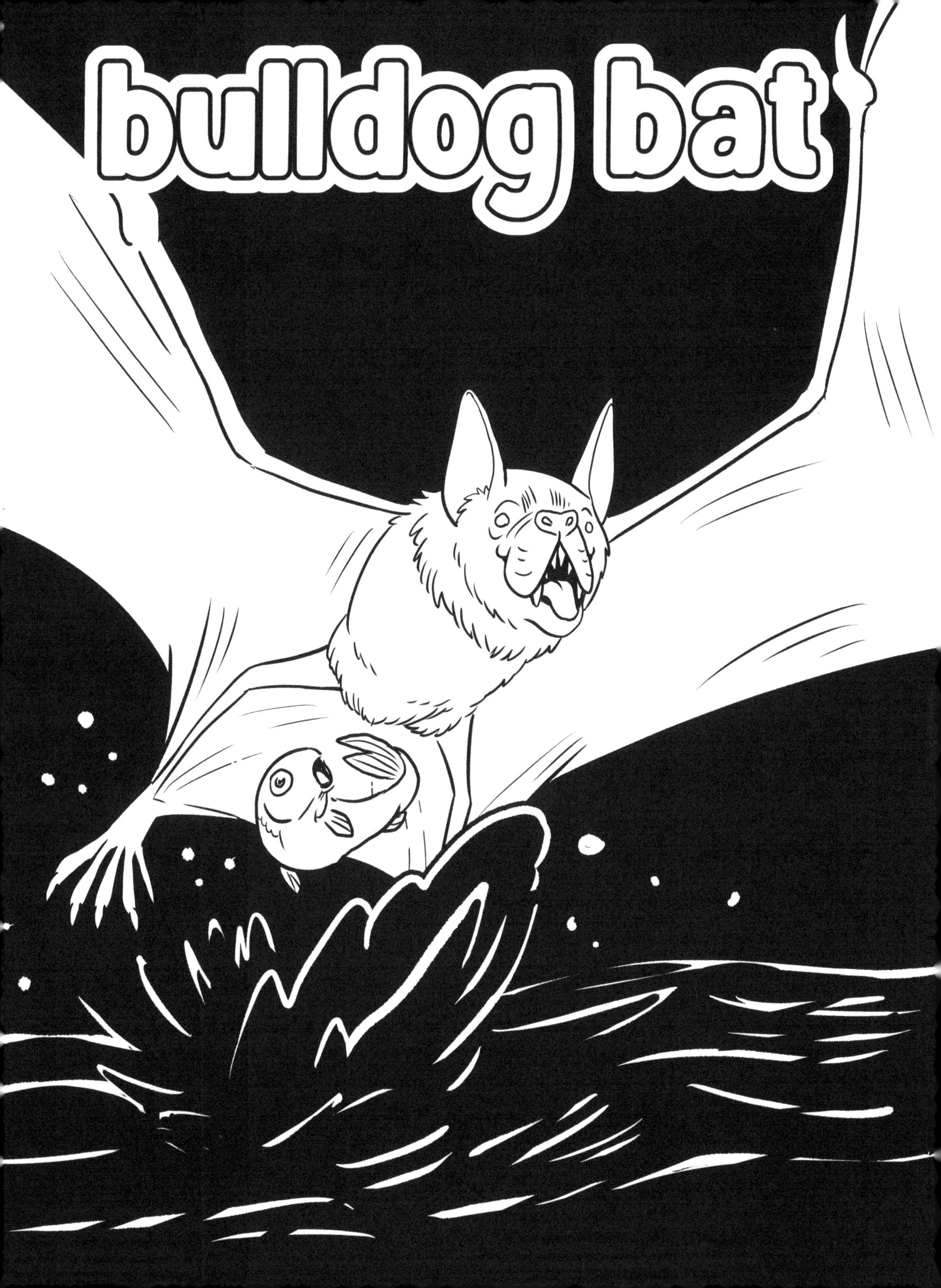

bulldog bat

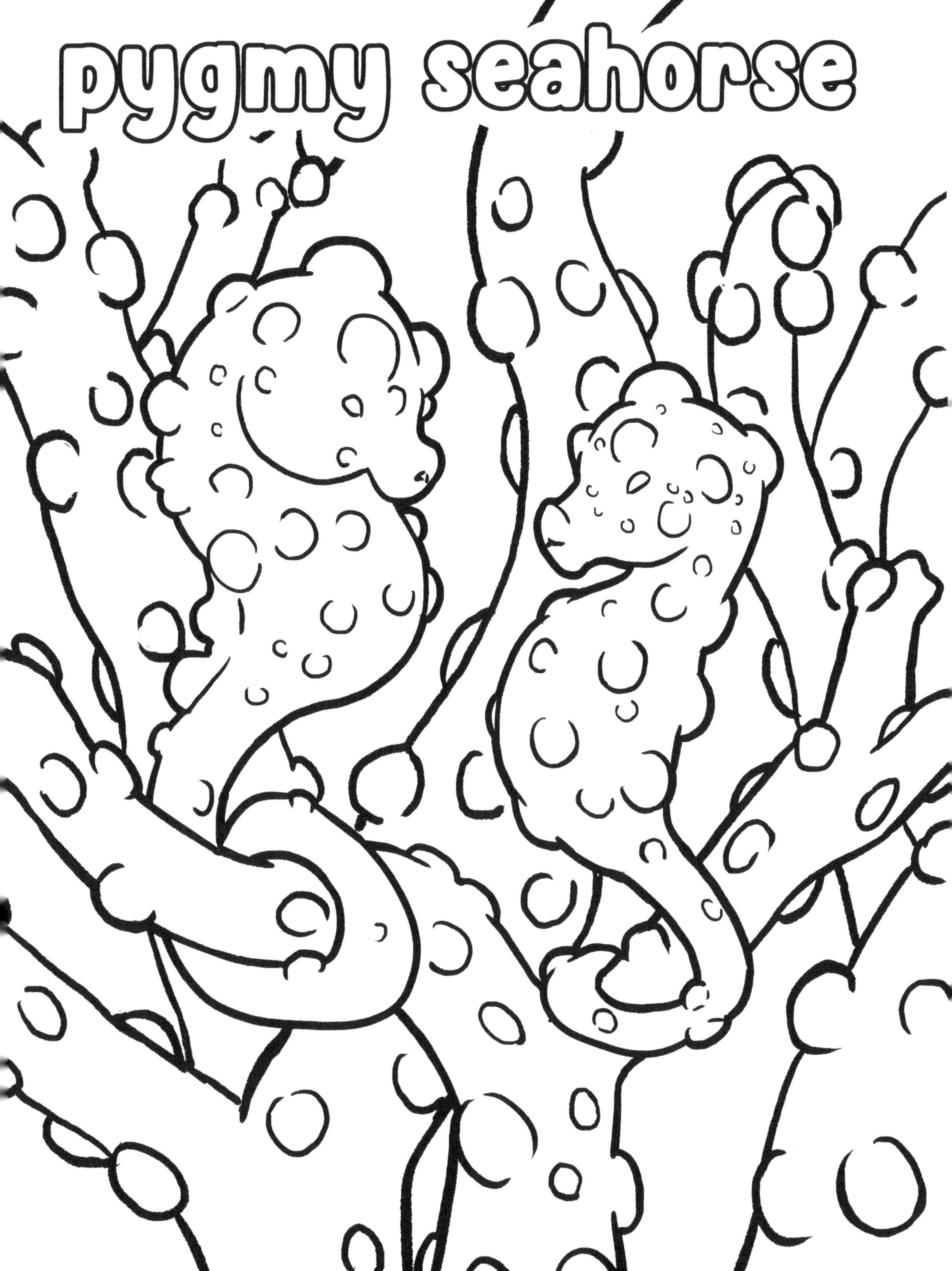
pygmy seahorse

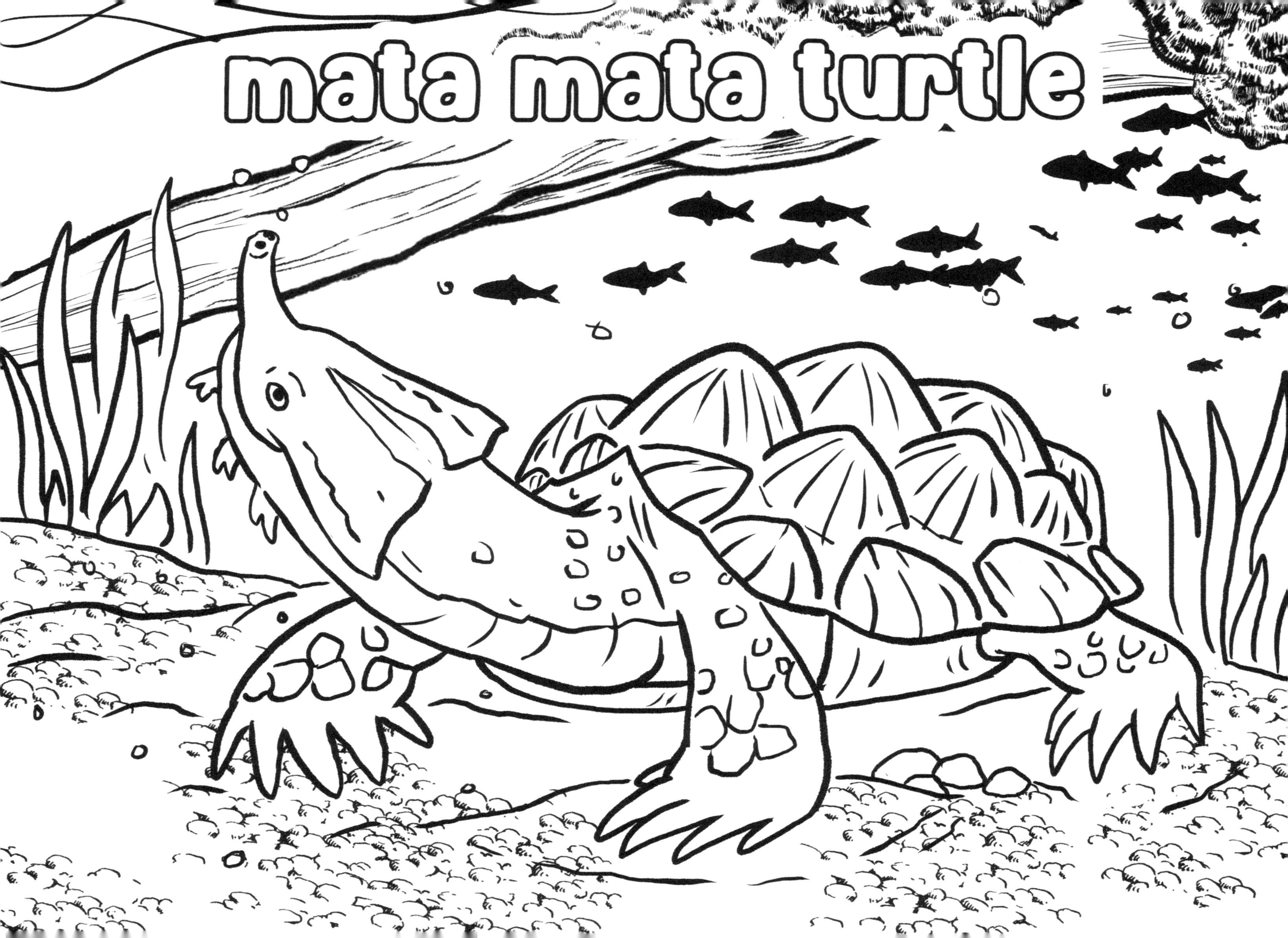
mata mata turtle

here's a color test page!

www.ingramcontent.com/pod-product-compliance
Ingram Content Group UK Ltd.
Pitfield, Milton Keynes, MK11 3LW, UK
UKHW062007290726
14090UKWH00022B/1442

9 798989 935536